# Cleo and Cindy

## What Two Dogs Taught Me About Unconditional Friendship

*To Jennifer, Rebecca & Tania; dog lovers like me!*

Jack Dempsey

*Jack Dempsey*

## Alpine
**PUBLICATIONS**

Loveland, Colorado

**Library of Congress Cataloging-in-Publication Data**

Dempsey, Jack, 1935-
Cleo and Cindy : what two dogs taught me about unconditional friendship
/ Jack Dempsey.
p. cm.
ISBN 1-57779-070-7
1. Dog--Biography. 2. Human-animal relationships. 3. Dempsey, Jack 1935- I. Title.

SF426.2.D46 2004
636.7'0887--dc22

2004062286

The information contained in this book is complete and accurate to the best of our
knowledge. All recommendations are made without guarantee on the part of the author
or Alpine Publications, Inc. The author and publisher disclaim any liability with the
use of this information.

This book is available at special quantity discounts for breeders and for club
promotions, premiums, or educational use. Write for details.

For the sake of simplicity, the terms "he" or "she" are sometimes used to identify an
animal or person. These are used in the generic sense only. No discrimination of any
kind is intended toward either sex.

Cover Design: Laura Newport
Editing: Betty J. McKinney, Deborah Helmers
Layout: Laura Newport

First printing September 2005

1 2 3 4 5 6 7 8 9 0

Printed in the United States of America.

# CONTENTS

**Preface** . . . . . . . . . . . . . . . . . . . . . . . . . . . . . . . . . . . . . . . . iv

**Foreword** . . . . . . . . . . . . . . . . . . . . . . . . . . . . . . . . . . . . . . . v

**The Start of Something Wonderful** . . . . . . . . . . . . . . . . . . 1
A tiny, gentle ball of fur—Cleo—brings excitement to a
man temporarily separated from his family.

**Cleo and Carolina** . . . . . . . . . . . . . . . . . . . . . . . . . . . . . . . 15
The man recognizes his "special" relationship with young
Cleo and shares her with his family.

**A Happy, Normal Lifestyle** . . . . . . . . . . . . . . . . . . . . . . . . . 25
The human/canine relationship provides daily joy for dog
and humans alike for years.

**Cindy Arrives** . . . . . . . . . . . . . . . . . . . . . . . . . . . . . . . . . . 37
An exuberant Cindy arrives, adding pep to life and more
than a little noise.

**Clouds on the Horizon** . . . . . . . . . . . . . . . . . . . . . . . . . . 47
While Cindy revels in life, Cleo's health slowly deteriorates.

**The Worst Day Ever** . . . . . . . . . . . . . . . . . . . . . . . . . . . . . 59
The family experiences the agony of putting Cleo down.

**Recovery and Reorientation** . . . . . . . . . . . . . . . . . . . . . . 61
The man becomes acutely aware of how pervasive man's
love of dogs is in society.

**Understanding It All** . . . . . . . . . . . . . . . . . . . . . . . . . . . . 75
The relationship between dog and man is understood in
the contexts of evolution, religion, memory and exciting
research on animal intelligence and the "unity of life."

**Into the Future** . . . . . . . . . . . . . . . . . . . . . . . . . . . . . . . . 87
Cindy continues to provide joy, and the memory of Cleo
is carefully preserved.

**About the Author** . . . . . . . . . . . . . . . . . . . . . . . . . . . . . . 95

iii

# PREFACE

This is a simple, happy story of a man's special relationship with two dogs.

There are no heroics in the story. Neither the man nor the dogs performed extraordinary services for each other. The dogs didn't wake the man to alert him to a fire or drive off an assaulting intruder. The man didn't impoverish himself to pay off humongous veterinary bills. It was simply a matter of a human and canines peacefully enjoying each other day after day, year after year.

It was, however, more than that. The man had owned many dogs and other pets before Cleo, then Cindy, arrived and he loved them all. But there was something . . . special . . . about his relationship with those two dogs. He found their companionship a daily delight to a degree not experienced before. His relationship with them rivaled in meaningfulness the finest relationships he had forged with human friends.

The realization of that startled the man, then stimulated him to try to understand how two different species could form a . . . friendship. His reading and thinking about that carried him into today's rapidly expanding scientific literature which is documenting that animals are much more like us than we thought, are much more intelligent than we thought, can do more than we thought and are more closely related genetically to humans than we thought. All of these findings help explain how these two species can bond to each other, because they are not as different from each other as we thought. And when the unique characteristics of an animal harmonize with the unique characteristics of a human, a *truly special* relationship becomes possible.

I am, of course, the man in the story. I have prepared this manuscript mainly to protect my memory of the now-departed Cleo and the still-living Cindy. But I have encountered many, many people who also have formed special relationships with all manner of pets and I realized that they, too, might enjoy my story. So here it is for those kindred souls. You and I have been blessed with one of life's most satisfying experiences.

*Jack Dempsey*
August 1, 2004

# FOREWORD

We need more of this kind of book about dogs.

The title, *CLEO AND CINDY: What Two Dogs Taught Me About Unconditional Friendship,* says it all. This is a love story that anyone who has loved a dog and been loved in return will appreciate.

We especially need this kind of story today because we hear of too many cases of Pit Bulls and other breeds attacking children and adults. I have no doubt that in the great majority of these cases, the dogs have been taught by their owners to be attack dogs. In some cases, of course, a vicious dog may have a genetic defect. Pit Bulls, for example, can be among the most affectionate and loving of dogs. Perhaps dogs can be bred to be hostile to humans, but that is certainly not the nature of dogs in general, no matter what the breed.

For example, last year I adopted an adorable seven-week-old puppy from my local animal shelter. He had been a stray, which means that someone had abandoned this helpless creature. Another someone, who cared about animals, brought him to the shelter. He was all black except for a white triangle on his little chest and white markings on the tips of his feet. The shelter people and I thought he was a "Lab Mix," mixed with what we did not know, perhaps a Border Collie?

As it turns out, this puppy, whose name is Charlie Brown and now about a year old, is huge and is a "Doberman Pinscher Mix." Dobermans are another breed with a reputation for ferocity. Not Charlie Brown. He is one of the sweetest dogs I have ever had the pleasure of knowing and falling in love with.

The point is that when dogs get reputations for viciousness, it usually is not their fault; rather, it is the way they have been raised and treated by their human owners. With the exception of undomesticated wolves, coyotes, perhaps hyenas, dingoes and the wild dogs of Africa, dogs are not naturally unpredictable or dangerous. In fact they have been bred by humans over thousands of years to be Man's Best Friend.

Some people don't like dogs. This is their loss. All over the world dogs are horribly mistreated and abused.

I live in the country, the beautiful rolling hills of northeast Pennsylvania along the equally beautiful Delaware River. This is dairy country and a dwindling number of my neighbors are dairy farmers, some of the best people in America. I'm sorry to say, however, sometimes they treat their cows much better than they treat their dogs. Too often when I pass a dairy farm, I see a dog tied up outside the barn. Most have a doghouse they can retreat to, some don't. At the very least, these dogs, which are social animals, must be terribly lonesome. They bark at everything that passes by. Perhaps that is what the farmers want the dog to be—a sort of alarm to let them know that the cows and calves might be threatened in some way. If that's the goal, there has to be a better way.

In my view, keeping a dog (almost always a mixed breed) tied up outside in all sorts of weather is cruel. But these farmers are not cruel—in fact, they are probably only doing what generations of their ancestors did.

There is a growing controversy about mixed-breeds versus purebred dogs. Obviously, breeders and the American Kennel Club vigorously defend the superiority of the pure breeds. It is true that the behavior and temperament of AKC dogs is more predictable, as is the way they look. If you buy a purebred Golden Retriever puppy, for example, you know what he's going to look like when he grows up. On the other hand, many purebred dogs are subject to all sorts of genetic diseases and defects. This is because they have been over-bred or even inbred.

Biologists Raymond and Lorna Coppinger have written a controversial book, *Dogs: A Startling New Understanding of Canine Origin, Behavior & Evolution*. They argue that purebred dogs may be headed for extinction because they are the offspring of such a small gene pool. And without new genes coming in, the gene pool gets smaller and smaller. The Coppingers come down on the side of mixed breeds, which has the AKC and its admirers up in arms. Other biologists dispute their theories and the battle goes on.

Personally, I have rarely met a dog I didn't like. We started out with Jenny, a beautiful Golden Retriever puppy. We bred her with a champion and she had nine wonderful puppies. We kept one of the female puppies, Mink, and then had both Jenny and Mink spayed at the proper time. Raising a litter of puppies to weaning age, when they can be sold or given away, is a *major*, time-consuming job. Both Goldens died when they were about ten years old, which is not unusual for this large breed. Smaller dogs tend to live longer.

When Mama Jenny died, daughter Mink went into major depression, getting to the point that she wouldn't eat. We thought that the only solution was to get a new puppy for Mink, as if we needed two big dogs. Maggie, a Lab of champion lines, arrived and within a day Mink snapped out of her depression and turned into "Mama Mink." Once you have two dogs, an adult and a puppy, you can never stop! Then the boyfriend of a neighbor's teenage daughter gave her a little Black Lab mix from a shelter, but her father would not let her keep it in their small apartment. Guess who felt they had to take in that puppy? Now we had three big dogs! The daughter's name was Angela, so the puppy became Angie. We had her spayed when she was old enough. Mink died first, of course. You could tell that Maggie and Angie missed Mink, but they had each other. When Maggie died, however, Angie was distraught. So we went to the shelter and got Charlie Brown.

I have loved all of our dogs, purebred and mixed breed. I think our "shelter dogs" may be a little brighter than the Goldens and Labs. In fact, Charlie Brown is too bright for his own good. When he's outside off leash, he runs into the woods and refuses to come back to you until he is good and ready. He is slowly getting better, but Mr. Brown is the most stubborn dog we've ever had.

I can't imagine a life without dogs. Someone said that when they died, they didn't want to go the heaven unless there were dogs up there.

I agree completely.

*George Page*

George Page is the creator and longtime host of PBS' *Nature* series. It has run continuously for over two decades, making it TV's longest running weekly natural history program. He is the author of *Inside the Animal Mind: A Groundbreaking Exploration of Animal Intelligence.* He now lives in retirement in rural northeast Pennsylvania. His love of the living world has inspired countless viewers and readers.

# The Start of
# Something Wonderful

It was Friday afternoon. I was driving home, not looking forward to another weekend alone in a big, empty house. I stopped here and there in search of anything that would kill time.

Then I saw her and something clicked. There she was, a little orange ball of fur, playfully and daintily prancing around, looking for something interesting to do, completely oblivious to the goings-on around her. Something inside me told me I had to hold her. I *needed* to hold that little ball of joy—I just had to.

I cradled her against my chest and she laid her head on my neck, motionless and cuddly. I melted. I knew I had to have her.

In the wink of an eye, I paid my fee and was driving home with my Golden Retriever puppy. I felt more excited than I had in a long, long time. Everything had happened so quickly I could scarcely believe it. Apparently I had had a need of which I was unaware and I recognized that this tiny ball of affection would fill it. Little did I know that I was in for one of the more significant relationships in my life.

It was a marvelous weekend. Far from being cowed by her new surroundings, my new obsession set out to explore all the recesses of her new home—and there were plenty of them. We owned a huge, three-story, 100-year-old house that was almost completely empty. Judy had already moved from Maryland to North Carolina and I had stayed behind to sell the house. Only the furnishings I absolutely needed remained.

The puppy knew none of that, however, just that she had all kinds of play space and a strange human she could play with any time she wanted. The human, of course, reveled in her frequent demands for attention. Oh, she was a little charmer, she was, and so beautiful. A modern day Cleopatra. Yes, I would call her Cleo.

I might just as well have called her Puddles. Lord Almighty, she seemed capable of going at will, a little here and a little there, usually a few inches *off* the newspapers I laid for her. She was so prolific that it actually seemed she could pee more than she drank.

But she was able to hold it all night. When I retired that first night, she sat on the floor and looked at me in a pitiful way. I am a large man and was reluctant to lift her to the bed for fear of squashing her during the night. But I couldn't leave my little Cleopatra alone on the floor and she became my regular nighttime companion. If something woke me, I could reach out and touch that little ball of soft fur, delighting in the experience of genuine affection between man and animal.

Waking in the morning became something of an adventure. Half-asleep, I would gobble Cleo up and rush her outside for her first pee of the day. She dutifully obliged every time.

Then I began a routine that would persist daily for over a decade. First pee done, I would dress, drive myself and Cleo to a local convenience store for a container of hot coffee, and then go to the high school grounds, which were free of traffic. I usually arose at 5 A.M., so we even beat the early dog walkers. The grounds were spacious, but there was sufficient illumination from street lights even in the dark, winter months to walk safely from one side to the other.

As I sipped my hot, delicious coffee, Cleo trotted along at a slow gait about ten yards from me. She seemed mostly absorbed with the odors in the grass, keeping her nose a few inches from the ground. She would check on me from time to time to assure herself that she was still close to me.

It was obvious Cleo thoroughly enjoyed these twenty-minute walks, even in the dead of winter and especially when she found a lost tennis ball in the grass. She actually seemed to prefer cold weather. And I relished the sight of this young animal being . . . herself. Two different species enjoying a common experience—I thought about this many, many times.

During the first few days of Cleo's entry into my life, I noticed several unusual personality characteristics. First and foremost, she was quiet. All the puppies I had previously owned or knew were quite capable of raising a racket, but Cleo never barked or whined. I only knew she was around by sight or when she physically demanded attention from me. It was most unusual. She was active in a dainty, gentle way, but she made no sound.

Her large, floppy ears also made it difficult to read her mood. They just sat there on either side of her head, immobile. Dogs like shepherds with smaller, upright ears signal their mood by positioning the ears straight up (alertness) or pinned back (cowed or submissive) with several shades in between. Not Cleo's ears.

She was the calmest puppy I had ever seen. No unrestrained outbursts of exuberance. No gleeful jumping up on me. No hyper-aggressive play. Just a continuous display of happy, curious, dainty behavior.

Only one thing dramatically changed her mood—loud noise. If a car outside backfired or a fire truck roared by, she would immediately rush over to me to be comforted. She would quiver all over and bury her head in my lap until she felt the danger was past. For her entire life, she would seek physical reassurance from me after any loud noise.

With that exception, it was difficult to read Cleo's emotions. She wasn't given to wild or obvious mood swings, she didn't bark, her ears never moved, her default attitude was playful curiosity. She was the same pleasant little creature all the time and I just loved her for it.

I had picked the perfect week for breaking in a puppy. I was working on several technical reports at home. Once a day I would drive into town to drop material off and pick up whatever new material was waiting for me. I took Cleo with me, of course, and she loved traveling by car. More than that, she didn't seem to mind being left alone for a few minutes while I made the drop-offs. This was a calm, secure little creature that, from the very start, exhibited every confidence that I would care for her and never abandon her and never, never hurt her. In less than a week, I became joyfully aware that I owned a truly unusual, totally wonderful little girl.

Golden Retriever pups and dogs come in various shades of tan and orange. All of them, however, are cuddly balls of fur. The pup on the right is very light tan and the one on the left, one shade darker. Cleo was one full shade darker still. This photo, © Don Ayres, appeared in the calendar *Playful Pals* (2002).

It almost was like she wasn't a dog. I found myself referring to myself as daddy and to her as my little girl. I've always bristled when people refer to a pet as "it." That's O.K. if you're referring to a stray cat—"it" must be lost—and you don't know the gender. But "it" depersonalizes a pet who believes *it* is a member of the family. Cleo was anything but an "it."

It's not extraordinary for a strong bond to develop between a puppy and her masters in the weeks following their meeting. But it's only now that I can appreciate how strong that bond between Cleo and me became because of my unusual life circumstances at the time. Most puppies join a family with several members, frequently including children and sometimes including other pets. The puppy interacts with everyone in the environment and no one human has total control of meeting the pet's needs.

That was not my situation. Never before had I lived alone, having moved directly from my parents' home to my apartment with Judy after our marriage. From the start we always had pets—dogs, cats, white mice and miscellaneous others. Little did I know that, when Judy moved to North Carolina and I stayed behind to sell the house, the sale would take three years in Maryland's down economy. Every other weekend I would take a load of furnishings down to North Carolina, so that the house I lived in became emptier and emptier.

The dogs went down shortly after Judy moved, leaving me with seven quiet cats. The silence in the empty house was eerie, so I bought two chatty finches, Hector and Homer, and enjoyed their incessant chirping. But Hector died and one of the cats somehow opened the cage door and got Homer. With Judy finally settled in North Carolina, I took the cats down to their new home. Then the

## THE AKC AND GOLDENS

The Golden Retriever breed was developed in Scotland in the late nineteenth century and was first registered in the United States by the American Kennel Club in November 1925. The AKC describes the breed as follows:

Goldens are easy to train and strong, but their most outstanding trait is character. They are outgoing and devoted companions for all sorts of people, happy and trusting. . . . [Renowned] for its reliable temperament, the Golden Retriever makes a great hunter, family pet or show dog. . . . The first three dogs of any breed to achieve the AKC Obedience Champion title, first available in July 1977, were all Golden Retrievers.

www.akc.org/breeds

Maryland house was not only totally silent, but completely still—not a blessed thing in it even moved. It was unreal. And unnerving. It wasn't that I wasn't busy. To maintain a cash flow until the house sold, I provided consulting services to local health departments across Maryland and conducted a study in several counties outside Richmond, Virginia. On alternating weekends when I didn't travel to North Carolina, I visited public gardens in seven mid-Atlantic states for a travel book I was writing as a hobby. Add it all up and I was traveling all the time, maintaining few continuous relationships and spending prodigious amounts of time writing technical reports and my garden travel book. I began to feel that only prisoners in solitary confinement were more isolated than I.

In short, you had a man accustomed to living with people and animals all day long and for his entire adult life. Then he finds himself suddenly and nearly completely isolated from daily contact with the human and animal world. The sale of the house that would have ended it all drags on for years. A need develops of which he is only partially conscious. And then along comes a cuddly, frolicy, affectionate puppy. The bond is instant, strong, exhilarating and, above all, permanent. And the puppy responds in like kind. An unusual situation and, for me, an unexpected one. What a wonderful solution to the problem! Cleo would enrich a dozen years of my life in a way I never dreamed possible and to a degree unequaled by a human outside my family. I don't know what my life would have been without her.

Cleo and I did have a common friend. It was a burnt-orange Nissan pickup truck with a king cab. It was my second pickup.

I bought my first pickup in the 1970s shortly after the Arabs shut off the oil and long gasoline lines formed all over the country. There had been talk of heating oil shortages, so a friend of mine and I went into action. We bought wood burning stoves, chain saws, splitting malls and wedges, and all the other paraphernalia one needs to heat a house with wood. He had a pickup which was essential to cart our cuttings home. When I saw how useful it was, I bought my own.

Prior to that time, I had never even thought of buying a pickup truck. Yes, a second friend of mine, a pediatrician, also had one, but somehow it wasn't . . . me. But I bought the truck anyhow and soon found it solved many problems. I could get sheets of plywood and other bulky materials home rather than wait days for delivery. At auctions, I could obtain large items like refrigerators for ridiculously small prices because no one else could transport them home. Its main use, however, consisted of hauling home the wood I cut down in the valley. Those were messy loads, but cleanup consisted simply of hosing out the bed.

With time, that tough little vehicle wore out. The only thing I hadn't liked about it was the small cab. So I bought a replacement truck with a king cab. There were fold-down seats behind the driver and passenger bucket seats; with the seats folded up, there was room in the rear of the cab that I found very useful. Additionally, I put sliding windows facing the bed, a hitch for dragging a camper and a detachable cap over the bed. I was ready for anything.

That second truck was the most dependable vehicle I ever owned. I drove it 284,000 miles, then gave it to my son who got some additional mileage out of it. It was nearing its last year of life when Cleo arrived. She made herself quite at home in it from the very start. Her favorite spot was on the floor behind the passenger seat where she assumed responsibility for a *very* important task. When I bought coffee in a paper cup on our travels together, Cleo determined that it was my responsibility to empty all the foul brown liquid in it, after which it was her responsibility to shred it behind my seat. And, wow, she was thorough; each cup was reduced methodically to a heap of tiny pieces.

After Cleo proudly polished off a cup, she would climb up front onto the passenger seat for a rest and a congratulatory pat from me. And for the rest of the trip she would alternate between the passenger seat and the crawl space behind it. I've always enjoyed driving, but watching Cleo amuse herself on our travels was a cherished extra treat.

I definitely wasn't living alone any longer.

And so it went over the first months. Cleo, my dependable truck and I wandered all over the mid-Atlantic states. During the week, I would take her with me to county health departments across the state if I would be in them for less than an hour and the weather was mild. On alternating weekends, I would take her to her future North Carolina home or to a public garden I was researching for my travel book. It was a relationship on the fly, and it was fun for both of us.

I soon learned that Cleo, although she didn't bark, was otherwise all mouth. She thoroughly enjoyed demolishing my paper coffee cups.

She equally enjoyed unlacing my shoes at any opportunity. She never met a morsel of food she didn't like. She thought God made hands for her to play tug-of-war with. And tennis balls were the best of all. Yes, tennis balls. It started with the balls she found during our morning walks at the high school. At first, her puppy mouth was too small for a ball, but she found she could get a tooth or two into the felt cover and parade proudly with it dangling from her mouth. Then she found it was fun to strip the felt cover completely off the ball. That would end the game, however; she had no interest in naked balls.

Enjoyable as the traveling was, the evenings were the best. I was on the go since 5 A.M. and forced myself to stop at 6 P.M. each day. After dinner for two, the cleanup and a brief walk outside, the final couple hours were ours. I would sit on the floor, pillow behind my back against the wall, and turn on the TV. I let Cleo choose whether she wanted to play with me, play with the many toys I had bought her or take a snooze.

Usually she wanted to play with me off and on, and her favorite pastime was tugging at my hands as I tried to pet and scratch her. At first I enjoyed it, too, but pretty soon her needlepoint teeth left my hands looking like hamburger—and they hurt. Moreover, Cleo was persistent. I tried sitting on my hands to protect them, which she thought was part of the game. She'd poke her paws under me and prod around for those delicious fingers. She'd tug at my sleeves, try to gain access from between my legs and generally explore any way she thought she could get at those hands.

We humans are supposed to be smart, however. I knew Cleo really liked tennis balls more than anything else, so I bought her three new ones to distract her. It worked. She rolled the balls around, chewed on them and made sure she played with all three of them. My hands gradually began to heal.

From time to time, I had to rescue the balls from under chairs and especially from under a rolling file. It had just enough clearance under it for tennis balls and Cleo found it difficult to retrieve them, so I helped. But half an hour later, the balls would be under things again and I had to help again.

Then I noticed something unusual. After I retrieved the balls, Cleo would play with them awhile, and then deliberately roll them under something, usually the file. With her usual persistence, she would work tirelessly to retrieve them. Sometimes she succeeded and sometimes I had to help. I wasn't sure how to interpret her behavior. Did she think recovering the balls was a really nifty part of the game or was she training me to be a retriever?

I still don't know.

Oh, those were completely enjoyable, totally relaxing evenings. They sure beat the heck out of living alone. It's embarrassing to admit that I rarely had had so much evening fun with my three wonderful kids. That was partly due to the fact that the three kids and two adults and multiple dogs and cats and maybe a visitor or two were involved in many different kinds of interactions and no one depended solely on any single one of them for amusement. Cleo and I had only each other, and we made the most of it.

On one of our early trips to North Carolina, I had a most unusual experience with Cleo. I had finished my coffee and she had dutifully shredded the cup. She crawled up onto the passenger-side bucket seat, as was her wont. Slowly, I became aware that she was staring at me.

That wasn't so strange. I've had both cats and other dogs stare at me for several seconds from time to time. Most often, it seemed, they were trying to determine whether I was about to feed them.

But Cleo continued to stare at me and I found it amusing. When I returned the stare several times, she didn't break it off as humans do because it's considered rude to stare. She just continued for several minutes, which is a long time.

Gradually I began to believe that she wasn't staring, she was studying me. We had been steady companions for about three months and she obviously found me a loving and interesting person. She was trying to *understand* me. She was *thinking*. I was thinking about her, too, and had been thinking about the animal kingdom for most of my adult life.

Drat! Young Cleo disliked being left behind in our trusty truck. Here her normally relaxed facial expression has become tense with displeasure. She believed it was her job to be with me all the time.

I had had almost no exposure to pets or other animals in my pre-college years. I was a menopause baby and by far the youngest in my family, and my parents were well past the family pet stage. My mom would frequently rave about a shepherd named Blackie that died when I was a toddler, but she showed no inclination to replace him with another dog. And she disliked cats, as my father did. My friends' families had no pets. Additionally, suburban life didn't expose me to farm animals or wildlife. Finally, I took physics and chemistry in high school, but no biology.

I was about as ignorant of fauna as a young adult could be. I had heard about evolution and Darwin and the search for the missing link and godless scientists, but it must not have seemed interesting because I had no opinion on the subject.

Then I took a college biology course. The early labs focused on squirmy little things under the microscope—a complete bore. Things got a little more interesting as we proceeded up to more complex life forms. We finally got to the turtle and I studied a diagram of its innards just before the lab started. We were studying circulatory systems that day. Something about the diagram looked familiar, so I turned to a diagram of human innards. What I saw so startled me that my loud exclamation of "Oh my God!" drew curious stares from my lab mates.

The circulatory system of the turtle looked incredibly similar to the circulatory system of a human! The innocence of ignorance was shattered forever.

The body shapes of apes and humans are so obviously similar that I could understand how scientists could theorize that we were descended from—or at least related to—apes. Turtles, however, didn't resemble humans in any obvious way. They were much, much smaller and had part of their skeletons outside their bodies, not totally on the inside like ours. Yet the similarities in the two circulatory systems were undeniable. That realization shook me up considerably. I invested some of my scarce pocket money in a book by a man who was both clergyman and paleontologist. He saw no great incompatibilities between theology and the scientific theory of evolution. One question kept nagging at me as I read: "If evolution didn't happen, why did God make it look like it had?"

Thus sensitized to the whole topic of the relationships among species, I took note of articles and TV programs that I would otherwise have ignored. I particularly recall one TV program about chimpanzees. It showed a chimp using a twig to ferret termites out of a log for a snack. Before then, it had been believed that only man used tools, but there on the TV screen was an animal using a tool. Amazing, the announcer exclaimed.

From that time on, I delighted in the steady stream of research findings that documented how animals possessed greater capabilities than had previously been known. I loved it. I found myself rooting for the animals.

So I had no trouble believing that my little Cleo was studying me, *thinking* about me, trying to *understand* me at a mental level above the generally accepted limitations of "dumb" animals.

Before that experience, I had spent much time studying Cleo. Our modern, hectic lifestyle deters most people from doing that. The family dog or cat is there to have something to pet, to give the kids something to play with and to elicit a giggle now and then at some antic. We're predisposed to like and own pets, but we don't *think* about them much.

Well, I did. Lying on the floor in the evening with no distractions from any other living thing, it was pleasant to dwell on the similarities between the two species.

The external similarities are so obvious. Four limbs each. The head, trunk and limbs in the same relative position. On the head, the

## CROWING

Although it was a surprise to find that chimps could use tools like us, it was downright astonishing to find that some birds, presumably not as smart as chimps, could do the same thing. Here's a newspaper account of one British experiment.

> Researchers were stunned recently by findings (published in the journal *Science*) on the conceptual abilities of New Caledonian crows. In controlled experiments, scientists at Oxford University reported that two birds named Betty and Abel were given a choice between using two tools, one a straight wire, the other a hooked wire, to snag a piece of meat from inside a tube. Both chose the hooked wire.

Both birds had used the tool, but Betty went further than her possessive mate.

> Abel, the more dominant male, then stole Betty's hook, leaving her with only a straight wire. Betty then used her beak to wedge the straight wire in a crack and bent it . . . to produce a hook. She then snagged the food from inside the tube.
>
> Jeremy Rifkin, *The Virginian-Pilot*, 9/7/03, p. J1

Way to go, Betty. She not only used a tool, she made her own!

same relative positions of two ears, two eyes, two nostrils and a mouth. From one of my courses in comparative vertebrate anatomy, I knew the internal anatomies were similar: basically the same musculo-skeletal, cardiovascular and digestive systems. But what I enjoyed most were the behavior similarities. Cleo yawned like me. Exhibited curiosity like me. Needed sleep. Played. Watched birds fly by. Had food preferences. Sneezed. Showed fear, affection, joy, fatigue. Felt pain. Separately eliminated urine and feces. All in all, we were so, so similar. Most people never think about that, but I did and savoring the inter-species similarities became part of my relationship with my little friend.

As the weeks and months passed, Cleo grew so slowly that I lost track of her maturation. It was then that another similarity between Cleo and humans emerged and I was unprepared for it.

I had her in the yard one day when a mid-sized dog from up the street came bounding onto my property. Oh, he was a good-looking, highly energetic young fellow and he waltzed right up to my little girl. I didn't understand the scenario immediately.

Then I watched Cleo's changed behavior in amazement. She began prancing around and wagging her tail furiously and running this way and that. She was flirting! There was my daughter behaving like a brazen hussy. Shameless! My daughter! Right in front of me! I couldn't believe it.

Well, I took her by the collar and led her inside PDQ. She came willingly, but she kept looking back over her shoulder. All at once it was very plain to see that my little girl had become a full-blown teenager. My oh my, how the time had flown.

My wife and I had already decided to have Cleo spayed rather than breed her. Between already having two other dogs and the unsettled times surrounding the move, we couldn't face the extra demands of a litter of puppies. Although I didn't want to submit Cleo to a painful procedure without my being there—since she was accustomed to being with me all the time—I reassured myself that I had boarded her for the day several times near Richmond and, on each return visit, she seemed happy to see the nice folks there again.

She handled the spaying fine. It was my first evidence that she tolerated pain well. And she relished all the attention she received at the clinic. Lord Almighty, I never met any person or any animal that craved human attention more than Cleo.

That experience came toward the end of our stay in Maryland. The house finally sold and it was time to enter a new phase of our relationship. Cleo had helped me through my period of isolation and I had showered her with as much attention as a human can. It was time to move on.

# Cleo and Carolina

Cleo's first visit to her future home on North Carolina's Outer Banks had been a resounding success—for her. Our cats, on the other hand, dived for cover when the new animal arrived and the dogs didn't know how to respond.

Cleo, however, was blessed with a wonderful personality characteristic. Instead of being intimidated by the new and unknown, she assumed that all new places and people were opportunities for enjoyment. So she marched into her future home and reveled in her first contact with new people and pets and toys. Judy loves all pets, so that relationship was warm from the start.

It was an opportunity to understand my little friend in new circumstances. Judy and I took her with us to a nearby public garden that required that pets be leashed. Since I had never leashed Cleo, I had no idea what her reaction would be. With her usual predisposition to expect the best out of every new experience, she seemed to think this was a new game. Apparently assuming that it was she who was walking us, not *vice versa*, she put every ounce of energy in her little body into it. I mean, she would have done a sled dog proud.

When we tried to rest periodically, she would have none of it. This was a really nifty new game, and she dragged us on with a total physical commitment. I'm a 200-pound man and she was still more puppy than juvenile, but my arms began to hurt from the continuous pull.

Cleo's easy adaptation to a leash helped me begin to understand the Golden Retriever breed. Several families in our new community owned them and walked them past our house. All of them were relaxed, friendly animals and looked very much alike.

15

## IN THE PARKING LOT

People everywhere have dogs, but I've never seen the equal of coastal North Carolina. Seemingly everybody has at least one and even seasonal vacationers bring theirs with them. It contributes a little joy during the occasional trip to the convenience store. Dog lovers can ooh! and aah! over the canines in the parked cars and trucks.

When I would leave young Cleo in my parked vehicle, she always sat in my bucket seat facing the steering wheel. She drew as much attention as the other dogs, maybe more. If I returned to my vehicle while people were admiring her in my seat, they would frequently ask in jest, "Do you let her drive?"

"No," I would reply, "I don't let her drive anymore. She already has six points."

And I began to notice that Goldens were on more TV commercials than any other breed. Two in the same week proved most enlightening. In the first, several teenage girls were on a slow walk through a park and a Golden was sauntering along with them. In the second one, four or five young boys were delighted with their dad's new van and were racing madly to get the best seats first. The Golden raced wildly with them, proudly securing his favorite position behind the driver.

Neither commercial featured the dogs; they were just part of the scene. Goldens like to consider themselves part of the gang. If the gang is just sauntering along aimlessly, so do they. If there's a frantic burst of activity, they rejoice in that, too. They tune in to the moods of their people and consider themselves full partners with them.

Shortly after those two commercials, there was a *60 Minutes* rerun in which Mike Wallace tried to interview an alleged underworld figure at his home. Although no one would answer the door, the family Golden was outside and assumed Mike was a new playmate. He jumped up on him to get attention and tried to engage Mike in play.

# HOWARD HUGE®

**"Howard went through the haunted house at the fair
and scared all of the people who work there."**

Dogs are everywhere in the media—movies, TV commercials, newspaper stories and magazines. Although Snoopy probably is the best known pooch, I've always enjoyed Howard Huge in *Parade Magazine*. He's a big, huggable creature who participates fully and humorously in his family's life. © 2004; reprinted courtesy of Bunny Hoest and *Parade Magazine*.

Apparently neither that dog nor the entire breed has an ounce of watchdog in them. They *love* people.

A few days later, I wondered why *60 Minutes* aired that encounter. Usually they just say so-and-so couldn't be reached for comment. But I bet the show's producers (and maybe Mike himself) loved Goldens and left the footage in just for fun.

Meanwhile, Cleo continued to make herself right at home during our alternate weekends in North Carolina, and the other pets quickly adjusted to this friendly addition to the family. I well remember one visit several months after the first one. I let Cleo in before I unloaded the truck. Then, as I carried the first armful of household items upstairs, I heard Judy exclaim, "Oh, Cleo, I didn't know you were here." When I reached the top of the stairs, I saw Cleo lying in the middle of the floor, peacefully chewing on a toy bone. The other pets were snoozing or doing nothing in particular, as usual. It was as though Cleo had been away a few minutes instead of two weeks. Silent as usual, she hadn't announced her arrival. More than that, when Judy did see Cleo, it didn't immediately register that the dog had just arrived because she was behaving as if she had been there all along. I still laugh when I recall that incident.

That was about the time I realized I needed a new vehicle. My wonderful truck had safely carried me over 280,000 miles and was on its last legs. My every-other-weekend transport of belongings had nearly emptied the Maryland house and I no longer needed the hauling capacity of a capped pickup. And Cleo had outgrown it.

When my little companion was a pup, she had no trouble alternating between the front passenger seat and the crawl space behind it. With time, however, her growth made it a tight fit. To make herself comfortable on our long trips, she would stretch out on the passenger seat and place her paws on my right leg with her rump against the passenger-side door. That brought her paws next to my five-on-the-floor gear shift. Since Cleo never, ever refused an opportunity to give or receive affection, every time I reached over to shift gears, my hand would take a licking.

As time wore on and Cleo grew still larger, even that adjustment didn't work. She began to lay both her paws and her head on my right leg. She continued to lick my hand every time I shifted and I returned the favor with a scratch or two on her head. Thus, the simple, automatic act of shifting gears became an exchange of affection repeated over and over, literally thousands of times. It completely changed the dull, unemotional mood of driving and created in me a sentimental attitude toward my cozy little truck.

It was only recently that I learned just how attached people can become to their vehicles. I was listening one Saturday morning to Click and Clack's National Public Radio show, *Car Talk*. A young woman called in to say that she had recently bought a 1947 Chevy pickup truck and had a problem she couldn't fix.

The brothers found it amusing that a young-sounding woman would buy such an ancient vehicle and asked her why. She answered, to their delight, that she was a welder. When they asked for clarification, she explained that she made metal lawn ornaments and such like and that she needed the carrying capacity for large items she brought home like old, rusty gates.

She continued to say that the old man she bought the truck from was the original owner and had kept it in good condition. "I felt terrible when I started to drive away. He was crying something awful. I felt so bad for him."

Even the usually zany brothers were touched. The old man had cared for that truck for five decades. The stressful separation, probably caused by financial need or failing health, completely crushed his composure.

It was good to hear that story because I had been feeling embarrassed at how sentimental I'd become about my truck. I hadn't had it for five decades, but I'd had it for one and, more importantly, it was full of memories. These made disposing of it all the more difficult.

But it was time. I continued taking Cleo out with me in the morning for a ride on the Outer Banks. The other two dogs, understandably, wanted to go, too, but there just wasn't enough room in the cab for three dogs. I needed a different type of vehicle. I decided on a minivan with two rear benches that folded flat, making a very nice platform. Three dogs could fit in there nicely and I would still have a fair amount of carrying space.

Cleo was a family dog in North Carolina from the start. Here's little black Candy enjoying the sights from my sun deck. Young Cleo, however, wonders what Judy is doing inside.

Fortunately, I didn't have to trade in the truck. My son said he wanted it and I gave it to him. That way, I was assured I would see it again from time to time. He eventually passed it on to someone else and I was spared a final separation experience.

Am I being too sentimental about a heap of assembled parts? Perhaps, but consider this: If I drove a vehicle eight hours a day every single day, it would take *two years* to reach the 280,000 miles I had attained in my truck. That means I spent a significant part of my life in that "heap of parts" and it always got me there. The fact that I drove it a decade instead of two years makes it all the more important in my life's history.

People develop feelings for all manner of inanimate things. They feel bad when a favorite hat wears out, when the class ring is lost, when the easy chair succumbs to time and when anything that gave good service over a long period dies. And we feel hurt when we give prized possessions to our kids or others and they fail to care for them properly. I can understand the ruptured feelings of the old man with the '47 Chevy. It was with him nearly his whole life and its probable fate with a metal-welding young adult may have seemed undeserved.

I've only recently come to appreciate the importance of memory. Think about it. Memory is the sum total of our lives up to now. We tap into it constantly without even thinking. We search it for names, phone numbers and places where we put things. Without it, we wouldn't know how to fry an egg, drive a car or even tie our shoes.

But it's the emotional memories that most enrich our lives. The feeling we had at graduation. Our newborn's first smile. A success at work. That magnificent vacation. Sometimes these memories pop into consciousness by themselves, elevating our mood. At other times, when our mind in not in constant reaction to environmental stimuli, we think back to some pleasant experience and enjoy it once again. People who don't frequently access their memories of their finest experiences really deserve pity. They are confining life-enjoyment to the experience of the moment which, most often, isn't all that memorable.

So I don't feel embarrassed by my sentimental feeling for anything, even a heap of parts. From time to time, I enjoy thinking back to the hours of otherwise dull traveling with Cleo's head and paws on my leg and other driving memories. I really liked that truck and I can enjoy the memory of it any time I want.

In time, Cleo would teach me even more about the importance of memory.

At about this point, I began thinking frequently about the very special relationship I had with Cleo and its similarities to relationships I had had with special humans over my lifetime. Although I had owned many fine pets and known dozens of impressive humans, only a few of those relationships deserved to be called special. It got me to wondering what makes some relationships "special."

With humans, obviously, it frequently begins with shared interests such as sports, work, music, travel, church duties, community involvement and pastimes such as bridge. Many relationships begin with a shared need, such as surviving a nasty boss, working on a common problem such as obesity or even keeping the crabgrass from taking over. Then there are the intangibles: we find ourselves immediately attracted to some, but not others, and are hard-pressed to fully understand why.

Almost always, however, time together seems essential for forming a special relationship. I think that's why family bonds become so strong. Let's face it, we don't choose all our family members and wouldn't particularly care to associate with some of them if they weren't family. Yet time together allows us to work through frictions and forge time-tested, live-together relationships that last indefinitely.

With non-relatives, it takes time to develop comparable mutual understanding and mutual trust, the cornerstones of a lasting, special relationship. I've formed casual relationships with many, many fine persons but lacked the opportunity to spend enough time with them for a special relationship. I'm sure every reader has experienced the same thing.

Outside my family, I've enjoyed only three special relationships that stood the test of time. Two were formed in adolescence and have survived to this day in spite of our living thousands of miles apart. And I've formed only one special relationship in my adult life that has survived physical separation.

All of the above seems equally true of pets. I've fortunately enjoyed many rewarding relationships with pets—dogs, cats, birds, mice and more. Yet only two were special enough to rival my human relationships in importance to me. I am referring, of course, to Cleo and—to be introduced later—Cindy.

## FAVORITE BREEDS

The American Kennel Club registers 150 different breeds. Here are the top five most frequently registered ones (in descending order), and some selected others.

1. Labrador Retrievers
2. Golden Retrievers
3. German Shepherds
4. Beagles
5. Dachshunds

15. Cocker Spaniels

23. Doberman Pinschers

32. Collies

68. Dalmations

90. Belgian Malinois

124. Greyhounds

143. Foxhounds (American)

Source: www.akc.org/breeds

When I found myself living alone in a large, empty, quiet house and performing job duties that were largely asocial, I *needed* a living relationship badly. Even a couple chirping birds helped because they moved, made some noise and needed me to feed and clean up after them. Any sort of cute puppy, of course, would be better still because I could interact with him and take him with me on short trips. From the start, however, I knew my little ball of fur would be much, much more than that.

We certainly had enough time together to develop an intensely close bond. Sometimes we were together nonstop for several days in a row. From Cleo's perspective, the environment was constantly changing. There was the large Maryland house, the truck, the high school, the places I walked her on our trips and the North Carolina house. Cleo undoubtedly believed home was where I was—I was the only constant in her environment. Cleo would have loved any family that bought her. But I think her intense presence with me and my nearly invariable readiness to respond to her needs helped shape and amplify her need to give and receive affection. When we played on the floor after dinner, I gave her as much attention as she gave me. Another type of master might have found her demands excessive and rebuffed her. That, in turn, might have reduced her interest in exchanging affection as she developed. Stated differently, she might have been *trained* to minimize her affectionate interchanges.

As Cleo grew, she outgrew her obsession with my hands and gradually substituted visiting me frequently for a loving scratch. Again, another type of owner might have given her a little pat on the head and that would be it for the evening. And that, in turn, might have further squashed her natural outgoing temperament.

Obviously, I didn't turn her away. When she approached me and lowered her head between my knees, I relished running my fingers through the wonderfully soft fur under her floppy ears. When she was satisfied, she would look up at me with the gentlest eyes I have ever seen, which was all the thanks I needed. Indeed, Cleo was the gentlest living creature I have ever known, and I believe I helped make her that way.

It was a very special relationship between Cleo and me. I wonder how many readers have experienced something equally special. Not just a good relationship with a pet—a *special* one, one that rivals the best human relationships you have had.

I wonder and I hope.

# A Happy, Normal Lifestyle

With the move to North Carolina complete, Judy and I faced a major reorientation. Among other things, I had a whole passel of pets to care for then and Judy added Cleo to her daily animal chores. I continued my morning ride with the three dogs and a cup of coffee; Judy added Cleo to her daily walk with the dogs. And Cleo was surrounded with more activity—human and animal—than she ever had been when living alone with me.

In the new surroundings, I learned several new things about Cleo. In addition to disliking noise, she disliked heat. Our Maryland house and yard had been shaded by huge oaks and other trees, but the North Carolina house was exposed to full sunlight. On the porch or in the yard in North Carolina, Cleo would always select a shady spot; then, when shifting shadows left her in sunlight, she would move to a new shady location. Her orange hair seemed to soak up sunlight, leaving her coat surprisingly warm to the touch.

Inside, Cleo quickly learned that the tiled downstairs floor was cooler than the carpeted upstairs. One day we couldn't find her upstairs or downstairs. We looked and looked and finally found her in the bathtub in the downstairs bathroom. That became her favorite spot when all else failed to cool her off. Clearly Cleo's comfort zone was many degrees below ours, meaning we had to turn on the air conditioner sooner for her than for us.

I also learned Cleo was a world-class hair shedder and, for some reason, it seemed she shed more in the van than in the house. I could thoroughly clean the van one Saturday, and by the next it would look like I hadn't vacuumed it in months. The van soon became known as our dog vehicle; neither Judy nor my friends were anxious to ride in it. When we brushed Cleo's coat, we got many huge balls of orange fur—but she still had enough in reserve for the van.

I had always known Cleo possessed a hearty appetite, but her love of food took off in North Carolina. She had many more sources of snacks there than alone with me. She enjoyed her usual twice-a-day meals, and Judy's helpings were more generous than mine. Both Judy and I snacked from time to time and Cleo always managed to be there for a few morsels. When the cats and other dogs didn't finish their portions, Cleo helped herself. Although she never became fat, she definitely filled out completely.

Cleo had a unique way of sponging morsels. If Judy and I were snacking, she would approach and stare at the food. Not at us, just the food. For minutes at a time. She wouldn't bark or jump on us or nudge us, just stare at the food as if it were the most wonderful sight in the world. We'd resist for a time, but we always weakened.

Cleo's human interactions quickly expanded beyond the family circle. She assumed the role of official greeter when beach visitors strolled, ran or otherwise passed by our home. In this one area Cleo said no to obedience. There were people to be greeted and that took precedence over everything else. She went to greet them all no matter how loud I hollered.

Cleo also developed a comical side to her personality. Sometimes on the floor and sometimes on the sofa, she would lie on her back, with all four legs pointed skyward, and wiggle back and forth to

Cleo matured into a pleasant, life-enjoying lady in her North Carolina home with many human and animal friends. Isn't she beautiful?

scratch her back. She punctuated this exercise with grunts and groans of sheer ecstasy. It was such an unabashed display of creature comfort that Judy and I enjoyed a laugh every time she did it.

Sometimes after performing her wriggling dance on the sofa, she would remain on her back and look around the room. For some reason, she enjoyed looking at everything upside down and Judy and I would laugh some more. She was such a clown!

That was Cleo in North Carolina. Stay cool. Share her fur with any and all surfaces. Eat everything in sight. Scratch her back. Mostly, though, greet every human being in sight like a long-lost friend.

The story of how we came to have a house on the Outer Banks of North Carolina is too long to be told here except in cursory manner. It's the story of how two city-raised people married and together gradually developed a love of nature, animals both wild and domesticated, nature photography and rural life. Weekend and summer vacations were routinely spent on trips to the wild from Vermont to Florida's Everglades. Lost animals, mainly dogs and cats, were regularly brought home by us and our three kids.

Early in our marriage, we had a Dachshund named Tina. When Judy rescued Checkers, our first cat, during Hurricane Agnes, Tina was indignant. She stomped around for days in sheer disgust. But we loved Checkers and soon it seemed like everybody in the family was bringing home a stray cat. Tina gradually adjusted to the inevitability of it all.

One day Judy called to me to look out the window at the driveway. There, incredibly, was Tina nosing a kitten toward the house. The kitten didn't really want to be nosed anywhere, especially by a dog. But Tina persisted and another "throw-away" was added to our menagerie. It seemed as if Tina had decided that since she couldn't stop us she'd join us, and so she brought home her own cat.

Although we vacationed all over the place, we found ourselves returning frequently to the Outer Banks and, during one trip, found a lot for sale that was too good to pass up. It was in an all-residential community, situated high enough to offer a breath-taking, panoramic view of the Atlantic Ocean three blocks away. Then we spent years collecting furnishings for our future home-away-from-home. After we finally built the house, we rented it out during prime summer season and visited it as frequently as we could at other times. We enjoyed the quiet solitude of the off-season, the fall waterfowl migration and the occasional visits to our property by deer, foxes, raccoons and a smattering of other wild creatures.

One spring weekend, I made a quick trip to North Carolina to prepare our cottage for summer rental. As I always did, I read the local papers which projected an entirely different set of interests than those found in urban dailies. I particularly enjoyed a story about some dolphins that were trying to push a whale off a sandbar after the receding tide had left her stranded on it. I also noticed an article on the recent passage of a North Carolina state bill which increased the ratio of guidance counselors to students statewide. Coincidentally, my wife had just completed her second master's in guidance counseling. On my way back to Maryland, I picked up application forms in the school system on the mainland just off the Outer Banks.

Judy excitedly completed the forms and was accepted in just a matter of weeks. We canceled the summer rentals at the cottage and started packing. Amazingly, from reading the newspaper article to moving Judy and our daughter Kathy down, the total elapsed time was less than three months! You can appreciate from that blitz of activity that we couldn't wait to live there.

Well, unfortunately, I did have to wait. I put the Maryland house up for sale and spent my free moments making it presentable and carting a truckload of belongings to North Carolina every other weekend. I had no way of knowing at the time that the house would take three years to sell. As I described earlier, it was the solitude of that vigil that eventually led to my purchase of Cleo for companionship.

When the house finally sold and I withdrew from my public health career, I spent the next years tinkering on the Outer Banks. I worked a couple years as a correspondent for the regional daily (something I had always wanted to do), did some work for the Red Cross, finished my public garden travel guide, wrote another book, did some volunteer work and generally stayed out of mischief. We added three rooms to the cottage in support of these activities. Although my pursuits did require frequent local travel, I did much of the work at home.

It was in this type of environment that Cleo and I began our new relationship that would last a decade. Three humans, three dogs, seven cats and a large assortment of wild mammals and migrating birds coexisted on a high ridge overlooking the Atlantic Ocean. If someone had told Judy and me at our wedding that we would finish our lives in such circumstances, we would have laughed and laughed and laughed.

For a decade, morning and evening routines varied not at all and daytime routines varied little. I would rise at 5 A.M. and be greeted immediately by Cleo. She and the other dogs followed me downstairs and into the yard for the morning pee, then into the van. I sipped coffee during the drive and the dogs enjoyed the morning sights or just snoozed. Judy walked them later in the day.

I think Cleo missed the pickup truck. The jump to the van's rear platform was just manageable for her. Although she could still squeeze through the front bucket seats to the passenger seat, it was just too cramped. So she established squatter's rights to the space just behind the passenger seat and the other dogs went to their own favorite locations. At ride's end, however, Cleo would move over behind my seat and stick her head out my opened door so that she could get at least *some* affection during the ride. And once inside the house, she would precede me up the stairs, stopping and turning halfway up so that I could reach down and scratch her tummy. She repeated that at the top of the stairs. Then, with her affection needs met and with Judy up by then, she would wander into the kitchen to see what was for breakfast.

Daytime routines varied a bit. In good weather, Cleo spent much of her time on the porch or in the yard, if we were working there. During winter, she snoozed quite a bit and hoped I would take her with me on those days I worked at home but had to go out on short errands. I always did unless it was bitter cold.

Evenings were the best. From six to nine, we would eat dinner, clean up, watch a little TV and usually have a snack. The humans and the animals were all together in one area, and everyone was pleasantly full. The animals seemed most relaxed and affectionate during those three hours. Cleo would make the rounds frequently, seeking morsels of food or affection from anyone willing. The day ended with the evening walk in the yard.

Those were relaxed years in which we interacted with dogs and cats intermittently throughout our waking hours. Our lives were immeasurably enriched by this constant interchange of affection between humans and other species.

Although we have never regretted our move to the Outer Banks, there have been some bumps in the road. The same Mother Nature that gave us awesome sunrises and clouds of migrating waterfowl also gave the area hurricanes, rabies, disease-bearing ticks, sand fleas that drove our pets nuts in the summer, sea nettles that made a dip in the ocean risky and various other unpleasant surprises. Also, pets have shorter life expectancies than humans and, given our large brood, we buried beloved little friends on a regular basis. Although each one gave us years of enjoyment compared to the final days of mourning, those days were painful, indeed.

But it was human beings who treated us to the extremes of agony and ecstasy, and most of them were at church. On the agony scale, my new pastor ranked close to the top. He was a young man and dedicated, intelligent, well-educated and completely inflexible. He was an arch-conservative who believed every word in the Bible came directly from God and was TRUTH itself. Not a single word in the Bible, he enjoyed saying, has ever been proven false. We should accept every word as "gospel."

He was particularly hostile to the notion of evolution and defended Genesis to a word. He believed that all of the scientific methods used to estimate the age of the earth, human remains and everything else were flawed. He calculated that creation occurred about 35,000 years ago. He said he disliked educated people because he couldn't teach them anything. On one Sunday, he began his sermon with, "There are some deluded persons here who believe our ancestors swung on trees. . . ." I came close to walking out of church, but didn't lest I embarrass my family.

Once, I shared my opinion with him that Genesis and evolution didn't seem incompatible to me. All Genesis says is that creation took place over a period of time instead of "poof, here it all is." Evolution says the same thing about the importance of time. If God used evolution as a means of creation, I suggested, who are we to say He didn't? Halfway through my first sentence, I saw his eyes glaze over. He had no intention of discussing the matter with me. He was all transmission, no reception.

## AOL ENTERS THE FRAY

AOL invites its subscribers to participate in a poll nearly every day. On June 16, 2003, it asked us to choose from alternative explanations for the origin of man. When I entered my choice, 197,790 other persons had already done the same. Here is how they voted on the question, "Was Charles Darwin right? Did humans evolve from apes?"

48%—No, God created humans separately from animals.

44%—Yes, the fossil evidence suggests that humans and apes share a common ancestor.

8%—"Not sure" or "No opinion"

Although that was not a scientific poll, it did support the notion that theological and scientific explanations have roughly equal followings. But isn't it a shame that people were forced into such a choice. One wonders how folks would have voted on the question, "Did God use evolution as a means of creation?"

There are many retired clergymen on the Outer Banks and, of course, their opinions on this subject run the entire gamut. I'm an expert neither in evolution nor in theology, but I take both quite seriously and I find the rivalry between science and religion very disturbing. It does not seem possible that differences will completely be resolved soon, if ever. That puts people like me squarely in the crossfire.

This particular tension abated somewhat when my pastor left to fill a position elsewhere. I wasn't disappointed in the least.

I sat down with my next pastor to discuss whether I should even stay in the church. The evidence supporting evolution was mounting almost daily to the degree that ignoring it altogether seemed ludicrous. If my views would make him or others in the congregation uncomfortable, perhaps it would be best if I just left.

The new pastor seemed completely unconcerned. "Jack," he said, "the Bible never was intended to be a biology textbook. It's supposed to help us form a spiritual relationship with God, which is something science can't study. And spiritual leaders shouldn't meddle in the affairs of science which they know little about. I don't see that your views should bother me or anyone else."

## OUR COUSINS, THE CHIMPS

On May 20, 2003, a startling news item out of Detroit received front page headlines in newspapers and other media across the country. Biologists at Wayne State University School of Medicine had provided ". . . new genetic evidence that lineages of chimps (currently *Pan troglodytes*) and humans (*Homo sapiens*) diverged so recently that chimps should be reclassed as *Homo troglodytes*. The move would make chimps full members of our genus. . . . With the advent of molecular techniques to compare similarities in our DNA starting in the 1960s, most experts have come to accept the fact that humans and chimps are [more closely related than chimps and other apes are]. Studies indicate that humans and chimps are between 95 and 98.5 percent genetically identical." (*National Geographic News,* May 20, 2003)

Reactions to this idea were quite diverse. Dave Addis, a columnist in the *Virginian-Pilot* newspaper, wondered how chimps felt about the whole thing. He fabricated an interview with one that didn't find the closer association complimentary: "You didn't see any [of us] monkeys working for Enron, did you? Or WorldCom?" (*Virginian-Pilot,* 5/21/03, p. B1)

However, I do know a person or two who undoubtedly saw no humor in the story.

It seemed like a very sensible variation on "Render to Caesar the things that are Caesar's and to God the things that are God's." I still go to church and I still believe in evolution. This reminds me of a chance encounter I had with a psychologist on a plane to Los Angeles. I asked him what he hoped to accomplish in his clinical work. He said many of his clients were hung up with some dysfunctional ways of thinking that kept them from moving on constructively. His job was to help them find ways of understanding things that allowed them to get on with their lives. It was a simplistic statement, but appealing.

I know many people who are caught between conflicting ideologies in science and religion, which leaves them in conflict in *both* camps. They don't feel confident enough to commit either way and get on with life. I empathize with these folks and hope they find a way resolve the conflict in their minds.

It was also in church that I got my first insight into how other people felt about Golden Retrievers. Up to then, I had never had a single conversation with another owner of a Golden.

That first interchange came, incongruously, in a Sunday morning Bible study class. I forget what piece of scripture we were discussing, but we drifted off subject and I found myself remarking that I wished I enjoyed life as much as my Golden Retriever did. Well, the mood of the entire group changed. With just a couple exceptions, one person after another told of how cherished their Golden or that of a relative had been and how devastated the entire family had been when the dog died. It was like a group therapy session. Next to last, the man to my left said he wished more Christians were as loving as his Golden. Finally, a man named Warren Davis said he knew several Goldens who were better Christians than most Christians he knew. Everyone laughed long and loud at that, and I still enjoy the memory of it.

(I've since wondered whether Warren changed his mind a couple years later when he bought a new Golden pup. The young dog had a need for exuberant play. His favorite pastime was grabbing one end of the toilet paper roll and racing jubilantly through the house. Warren definitely wasn't amused.)

As I settled into my new North Carolina lifestyle, I relieved Judy of some of her round-the-house chores and she relieved me of some of mine, especially food preparation and walking the dogs. This division of labor left me with a less intense relationship with Cleo than I had had in Maryland. She caught on quickly, recognizing that Judy fed and walked her and that I took her on rides and played catch with her. Her mouth had grown large enough to catch a tennis ball and she became quite good at it.

But then I noticed that my food-loving little girl was spending more time with Judy than with me, even sleeping at the foot of her bed. I found myself becoming jealous. Had my intense relationship with Cleo in Maryland been all on my part? She really hadn't had any other alternative. Would she switch loyalties to whoever fed her?

The next electrical storm brought the answer. At the first peal of thunder, she raced immediately to me and buried her head in my lap. She repeated that in all thunderstorms, if summer revelers set off fireworks and when planes buzzed too low. If the noises occurred after I retired, she would plop next to my bed so I could place my hand on her to reassure her. If I was sleeping through some noise, she would jump on the bed for physical contact.

As I reassured her, so she reassured me. When affection and food were concerned, Cleo would cozy up to just about anyone. But when she felt threatened, she made a beeline to me. She still was *my* little girl.

She reassured me in many other little ways, most interestingly when Sam came to visit. Now, Cleo was a people dog. It wasn't that she had no interest in the companionship of other dogs, but they ranked a distant second to people. Sam was my daughter's dog whose physical capabilities had become legendary. My son-in-law had forewarned me that gentle Sam was also boisterous Sam. If he was bent on running somewhere and a bush was in the way, he just plowed right through it "as if it wasn't there." With that warning, I wasn't sure how Sam and my three would mix.

Well, it was a real hoot. At first there was a wary get-acquainted period with a lot of sniffing. Following that, all four dogs behaved remarkably well for a long time. At some point, however, Sam decided the party was awfully dull, so he challenged my three to a race. He dashed this way and that way and around trees and under the stairs—all at breakneck speed. My dogs didn't know what to make of it. Then Sam took off around the side of the house, out of sight. My three huddled together, waiting for him to re-emerge. But Sam circled the entire house and startled them from behind. That got the adrenaline going. The three dogs took off after Sam as he started his second romp around the house.

When Sam came into view again, my three were far behind. Little Candy had had enough and plopped down on the driveway. Cleo and Chelsea started around for their second time. Moments later, an exhausted Cleo dropped next to Candy, but Chelsea kept going. She didn't reappear for the longest time, but finally came staggering around the corner and just plain collapsed. Sam had lapped her at least twice. He took a victory lap around the house before standing proudly amidst admiring humans and canines. My three dogs stared at him in disbelief. They hadn't seen that much excitement in memory.

About that time, Judy asked me to drive to the store for something. As I walked to my van, I wondered if Cleo would come along as usual. She was having a great time with Sam and I thought she might want to stay.

Cleo found herself in conflict. She was almost exactly between Sam and me, about twenty feet from each of us. She looked at Sam, then at me, then back and forth several times. Then she just stood there, not looking at either of us. She was *thinking*, trying to make a choice. My daughter doubled over with laughter at the sight of my Golden's effort to make up her mind.

Finally, Cleo decided. She galloped decisively over to me and hopped into the van. I was still "top dog" in her book. It was one of the nicest compliments anyone ever paid me.

# Cindy Arrives

The jump up to the van's platform presented a bit of a challenge even for a large dog. At first, Cleo made it most of the time, but one day she missed several times in a row. Apparently she felt she wasn't up to it that day and just sat on the driveway, staring into the van. I pulled her up to a standing position, lifted her front paws to the platform, then got behind and lifted her rump up.

We've all met people whose pride prevents them from accepting help. Well, Cleo wasn't like that. She thought being boosted into the van was very nice, thank you. So, from that day on, she waited patiently every day for me to help her. And I did.

At the time, I didn't recognize the experience as an early sign of aging. I thought Cleo was probably gaining too much weight. But then other signs began to appear. She lost interest in playing catch with me. She still enjoyed chomping on tennis balls but she gradually stopped bringing them to me to toss to her.

More puzzling was her occasional failure to greet me first thing in the morning and to follow me downstairs and out for her ride. My study is on the ground floor and I would busy myself with administrivia until she finally made it down. I didn't realize what was behind this behavioral change.

The first irrefutable sign of aging was the graying of her snout. Golden Retrievers generally start graying there sometime in middle to late middle age and it proceeds gradually from then on. Obviously I wasn't happy to see it because I had never seriously considered the fact that I wouldn't have my little girl forever. Yet she was in good health, so I put that consideration on the back burner.

It was at this time that a tornado hit the house. No, not one of Mother Nature's. It had four legs and it arrived without warning. I was sitting on the sofa late one afternoon when Judy returned from school. Through the sliding glass door, I could see a dog with her and knew instantly we had a new pet. It looked a little like a juvenile German Shepherd. When the door opened, the newcomer looked at me and, without the slightest hesitation, crossed the room quickly, jumped on the sofa and leaned against me for protection. She was terrified and for good reason. Cleo and Chelsea were in plain sight and a couple cats were diving for cover. I put my arm around the trembling animal, which she accepted completely, snuggling up even closer for protection. She made no move while Judy explained the situation.

Judy had seen the animal hiding under a school bus that morning. She offered her food and water, which the dog accepted eagerly, but she refused to leave the protective covering of the bus. No one in the school knew anything about her, but they were not surprised. It was common practice in that county for people to drop off unwanted animals at the school, hoping one of the kids or employees would adopt them. Perhaps they thought doing so was kinder than taking the pets to the shelter to be euthanized. A severed stub on the shepherd's collar, where tags apparently had been attached, suggested that she had met this fate. When the school buses started rolling at the end of the day, the dog's very survival was threatened. Judy just couldn't leave the terrified animal there, so she brought her home.

As Judy talked, I looked at Cleo and felt terribly guilty. Normally relaxed, she had stiffened and stared at the animal and me in utter disbelief. *Her* master was cuddling a strange animal. Bad as I felt, I just couldn't push a distraught animal away.

I had seen that look on Cleo's face only once before. When I was walking her up the road a few years earlier, I heard the roar of a truck behind me. After I saw that the idiot driving it was speeding, I called to Cleo to move onto the shoulder with me. Unaware of the danger, she was slow to respond and actually drifted a little farther into the street. I panicked, slapped her behind and forcefully shoved her toward the shoulder. It was the first and only time I ever slapped her. She bolted about ten feet onto the shoulder, turned and looked at me with an expression of pained disbelief. I had done the unthinkable. Somehow, knowing that I had done what I had to didn't help. I had introduced an ugly experience into our relationship that Cleo simply did not understand. She forgave me after I showered her with affection during the rest of the day, but experiences like that stay tucked away in the brain. I had hoped I would never see that expression on her face again, but there it was as I comforted the terrified stranger. Once again my little girl—then a grown lady—forgave me, but my stomach still tightens every time I recall that look of agony on Cleo's face.

For a solid week, Cindy—we named her that after we determined her sex—followed me every single place I went, twenty-four hours a day. I was her security blanket. She was very slow to accept that Judy and the other animals were no threat to her. Only then did her personality begin to emerge.

Cindy was a beautiful young dog, apparently about nine months old and about two-thirds the size of a German Shepherd. We assumed she was a mixed breed. Her coat was a light brown except for some black fur on her ears and snout.

She must have led a restricted life before Judy brought her home. The first time I took her downstairs, she halted at each step, apparently never having negotiated steps before. She tried to run right through a sliding glass door, as though she had never seen one. She was threatened by all pets; it seemed likely that she had been an "only dog" before. The vet said she had been on her own awhile, possibly meaning that it took some time for her to find refuge at the school or that she had been kept outside. But she was obviously very intelligent, athletic and hyperactive. In about a week, she could round the sofa, hit the stairs in full stride and dash down them at breakneck speed. She was also a bit phobic, however. Her collision with the sliding glass door must have been quite painful because she frequently refused to pass through the doorway until someone else did so first— she was never sure whether the glass barrier was present or not.

She also was very possessive. For weeks, every time I tried to give Cleo some affection to assure her of my loyalty, Cindy would howl pitifully. I was her savior and she wanted me all to herself. Since we had a houseful of pets, all in need of love, she gradually came to tolerate shared affection, but even at this writing she still occasionally pushes other animals aside to corner my attention. Cleo *wanted* a great deal of affection; Cindy *needed* it. Cleo took affection from everybody; Cindy took it only from me and, later, Judy and Kathy. As time passed, it became ever clearer that Cleo and Cindy had virtually nothing in common. Absolutely nothing. They were as different as two dogs can be. Consider expressiveness: Cleo was nearly always nonvocal; Cindy nearly always spoke. She possessed the largest assortment of barks,

Although Cleo welcomed all visitors to our home enthusiastically, it took Cindy awhile to decide whether a visitor was friend or foe. This photo was taken when my son, Paul, visited for the first time and Cindy still hadn't made up her mind about him. Judy found the situation highly amusing.

whines, yaps, growls, cries and pleading sonatas I have ever encountered in a dog. If ever a dog tried to communicate vocally, it was she.

Then there were the ears. Cleo's floppy ears just sat there . . . all the time. Cindy's shepherd-like ears constantly alternated from straight up (fully alert) to straight back (submissive, threatened) with countless "neutral" positions in between.

In body posture and activity level, Cleo was always relaxed. Cindy could relax too, but she sprang to attention at the slightest stimulus.

Overall, it was difficult to detect changes in Cleo's mood, but that didn't matter much because her mood was remarkably stable. Cindy's mood, in contrast, was highly volatile and her vocalizations, ear positions and body postures made her emotions an open book.

The dissimilarities continue. Cleo feared loud noises; Cindy tolerated them remarkably well—she even slept through thunderstorms. Cleo ate everything in sight; Cindy was a finicky eater, sometimes leaving her meals untouched for hours. Cleo's attention focused on people; Cindy reacted to *everything*.

The two dissimilar dogs, however, did have one thing in common: they both were *my* dogs. Their affection for, and loyalty toward, me was awesome. Judy and I have had many dogs in our married life, but none had been *my* dog. The others were family dogs or formed a primary relationship with Judy. Cleo adopted me because I was the only human in her early life; Cindy initially bonded to me for protection and that foundation persisted. Like Cleo before her, Cindy came to accept everybody—humans and animals—in the house. And, like Cleo before her, her primary relationship remained with me. I felt very complimented, indeed. I worked hard at not letting these two dogs down.

I've always been impressed with how much animals teach each other. They are referred to as "dumb animals" because they are supposedly driven by instincts rather than conscious intelligence. Yet, throughout my life, one scientific report after another has documented that animals have far more conscious intelligence than previously thought, are much more similar to us than we thought and teach each other more than we thought. Stated differently, we humans don't know as much as we thought.

I was particularly impressed with a report on chimpanzees a couple decades ago. Some researchers studied how much sign language they could teach chimps. When the study was completed (it was highly successful), they stopped reinforcing the signs the chimps had mastered. To their surprise, the chimps continued to communicate with each other anyhow. And to their astonishment, the chimps taught the sign language later to babies born after the study. Isn't that interesting?

So I should have been prepared for a comparable experience after our move to North Carolina. We took two old dogs with us. One was a small, black mixed-breed, Candy, whom I saved from freezing to death in a supermarket parking lot. And there was Lady, whom my daughter had similarly rescued.

Little Candy was quite excitable and very territorial. She intensely disliked a neighborhood dog who came calling when he could escape his yard. The owner was a responsible man who didn't want his dog roaming the neighborhood. When he found the dog gone, he knew where to bring his pickup truck to retrieve him. However, the man also enjoyed going for a drive and taking the dog with him in the truck's bed, where Candy could see and hear him. The truck had a noisy diesel engine that Candy could hear a block away, setting her into a barking frenzy before it even came into sight. Lady soon learned from Candy how to identify the dog's truck by sound, and she barked lustily too, well before it came into sight. We named the truck the Hated Chevy because we thought that's what the dogs would call it.

With time, the man's dog died but not the truck. No matter, the dogs still barked every time they heard it coming. Then Lady died and we added Chelsea, a Bassett Hound. Chelsea had never met the offending dog, but learned from Candy that the Hated Chevy's sound portended something awful, so she also started barking at its approaching sound.

Then I arrived with Cleo, a dog that didn't bark at all, didn't even like noise and had never met the dog that started the ruckus in the first place. Through her juvenile period, she would rush to the porch with the others to see what the problem was, but kept silent. As an adult, however, she finally concluded the other two dogs might be right about the Hated Chevy, so she chimed in. It wasn't really a bark. It was a soft, almost gentle *wooo-wooo* that wouldn't scare a soul. But it made her one of the gang and she seemed happy.

When little Candy died, Chelsea kept up the good work with Cleo sometimes adding harmony. When Cindy arrived, neither Chelsea nor Cleo knew why they hated the Chevy, but Cindy never needed a reason to sound off. She quickly became adept at hearing the truck from afar and dutifully barked it out of sight. When Chelsea eventually died, Cindy carried the torch alone because Cleo had tired of it all and just ignored the whole thing. To this day, Cindy still protects us from the Hated Chevy.

Thus, dogs have communicated across three generations. It's not an earth-shaking phenomenon, but I find it interesting, albeit a little hard on the ears.

Of our many dogs, Cindy was the first that worried us. She was hyper-alert, easily threatened and responded to threat aggressively. We began to wonder whether her original owner had been a policeman who botched the training of a hyperactive dog so badly that he dumped her at the school without tags and told everybody she ran away. That suspicion was intensified later when we learned Cindy was a pure-bred

Belgian Malinois, a sheepherding breed frequently used in police work. We decided early on to keep her leashed at all times when outside.

One day I was in the yard with Cleo and Cindy when an elderly man walked by. I had leashes on both dogs but was holding only Cindy's. As expected, Cleo took off to greet the stranger. When the man saw the leash on her, he assumed she had gotten free from me. As I approached with Cindy to retrieve Cleo, the man stomped on Cleo's leash to hold her there for me. Apparently Cindy thought he was trying to kick Cleo and she lunged at him. I held her back forcibly. Although the man was startled, he still tried to help by picking up Cleo's leash and taking a step toward me. Cindy lunged again and I barely held her back. Cindy was not barking; she meant business. I called to the man to go on; he did so; I was shaking as I

## THE MALINOIS

The Belgian Shepherds were developed in the nineteenth century in, of course, Belgium. The American Kennel Club recognized the first of the breed in 1911. The Malinois is one of four varieties recognized by the Club. Here are excerpts of the AKC's description of the Belgian Malinois.

> The Belgian Malinois [has] an exceedingly proud carriage of the head and neck. The dog is strong, agile, well muscled, alert and full of life. . . . [The female] has a distinctly feminine look. . . . The [gait] is smooth, free and easy, seemingly never tiring. . . . The dog may be reserved with strangers but is affectionate with his own people. He is naturally protective of his owner's person and property. . . .
>
> www.akc.org/breeds

The description "full of life" may understate Cindy's dynamic temperament and definitely misses the mark with "reserved with strangers." Otherwise, that's my Cindy!

dragged both dogs inside. I didn't know whether Cindy was only trying to protect Cleo and me or whether she was a danger to any passerby.

Not long after that, I tripped on my porch stairs and dropped Cindy's leash. She thought that was a great opportunity to gallop up the street to see what was there. Even though I had a badly bruised knee, I tore after her in mortal dread of what she might do if she encountered anyone.

My worst fears were realized. A man in a pickup truck, of all things, saw her running with the leash dragging, stopped and went to retrieve her. I froze in terror as I saw him bend down and grab the leash. Then it happened—Cindy wagged her tail. She offered no resistance as he brought her back to me. Shaking, but relieved, I brought her back to the yard. She didn't resist a bit. She had enjoyed a little romp and was quite happy to be retrieved.

Although that incident proved Cindy would not attack a human without provocation, we still were wary. The next test came several months later when Judy brought another throw-away home from school. This one was a cat, all white, terrified and living under the school's air conditioner. Judy had fed her every day to keep her alive, but vacation was near, meaning the animal might starve to death. On the last day of school, therefore, she brought the cat home. And, a few weeks later we learned she was—you guessed it—pregnant. At the appropriate time, we built a pen in the living room for Angel, as we called her, into which she promptly jumped and where she presented the world with three kittens.

The pen was high enough to keep the kittens in and the dogs out, but low enough that Cindy could peer into it and watch the kittens. Cleo, the people dog, just ignored the whole thing.

Cindy would stare down at the squirming balls of fur for long periods of time. We had no idea what her intentions were and we dreaded the day we'd have to find out. Hesitantly, when that day came, we removed the sides of the pen and held our breaths. We didn't know what would happen.

*Nothing* happened. The kittens frolicked out; Cindy stared with great interest, wagging her tail. That was it. Our concerns had been groundless.

One of the kittens, Rascal, was particularly boisterous. When she had been in the pen, I suspect she found that strange head staring down at her as interesting as Cindy had found her. So she followed Cindy around, trying to play with her. Cindy didn't know what to do.

Sure, she found the little creature interesting, but she didn't want to *play* with it. At first she just walked away, but Rascal pursued. Gradually, she began to tolerate the little dynamo, even when it grew up and began wrestling with Cindy. We have a photo of the two of them cuddled up, snoozing together. We had our very own odd couple.

This is not to say that we needed to keep a minute-to-minute watch over a potentially destructive dog. No, in fact, Cindy was utterly delightful ninety-nine percent of the time. She was, and is, the most playful dog we've ever had. After Chelsea died, she tried frequently to engage Cleo in play. She had a favorite toy—a stuffed animal that she enjoyed chewing on, but stopped short at ripping apart. She would offer it to Cleo for a gentle tug-of-war. Cleo made a few feeble attempts to accommodate, but she really had no interest in that toy. Cindy, in turn, tried to play with Cleo's tennis balls, but she didn't find them all that enjoyable and she couldn't catch one worth a darn. When Cindy tried to mount Cleo from behind in a playful outburst of exuberance, Cleo simply sank to the floor, which ended it. Nonetheless, they seemed to enjoy each other and worked out their own routines. For the morning ride, Cindy always entered the van first and Cleo always exited it first. Back inside the house, Cleo would precede me up the stairs and Cindy would follow. They were quite compatible, but Cindy was far more interested in an interactive relationship than Cleo.

There was also a very strong comedic side to Cindy. She was intensely interested in every single activity and wanted to be in the middle of it. During the morning ride while Cleo napped, Cindy sat in the back and looked this way and that, interested in everything she could see; I enjoyed glancing at her through the rearview mirror. She snoozed on the sofa just like I do—head on the pillow. If a fly got in the house, she followed it around. It was fun watching her because she was so unpredictable, relished life so much and was so expressive. Her confusion the first time she saw a human on a bicycle sent me into fits of laughter. She would follow a bug across the driveway with intense interest. She was, indeed, a *bon vivant*.

She also understood routines and her rights to them. When it was time for Judy to take her on the morning walk and she delayed,

We have two sofas facing each other. I claim one as mine and Cindy claims the other. She has such a regal look about her.

Cindy would badger her with a yodeling series of barks, yaps and pleadings until she got her way.

If either Judy or I came home at the expected time, we were greeted with boundless affection. But if we came home later than Cindy thought appropriate, we received a sort of yodeling scolding.

All in all, we weren't thrilled with Cindy's incessant noise and we were wary of her aggressiveness, but she was such an amusing dog we couldn't stay angry with her for long. She was something special.

Cleo and Cindy—an outstanding pair!

And so it went on for years. Two magnificent dogs devoted to me. Cats and kittens all over the house. Fish and frogs in our two ponds. Visits from deer, raccoons, foxes, squirrels and rabbits. And, to remind us we weren't in paradise, flies and ticks and mosquitoes and bats and hurricanes. We enjoyed it, indeed. . . . Well, most of it.

# Clouds on the Horizon

Joyful as it was to own two special dogs, albeit with totally different personalities, that were equally and completely devoted to me, their lives were going in opposite directions. Cleo became gradually more sedentary in her adult life. In contrast, the ever-active but maturing Cindy relaxed and considered herself an essential component of all she could see in the house, in the yard, in the surrounding community. She claimed as hers all that she could see.

I worried about Cleo. Although stocky, she wasn't fat. Yet something was wrong. She never complained to us about anything and couldn't even if she wished. But something was wrong.

Judy saw it first. There was something wrong with her right upper lip.

It was cancer.

The English language provides no words that describe the bottomless feeling in my stomach at that discovery nor the boundless exultation I felt at the successful surgery, so I won't even try. I can only say my emotions fluctuated more wildly in that month than they had in memory. Yet, even with a successful outcome of surgery, something was still wrong. I never dreamed it was something she shared with me.

Meanwhile, I had encountered my own crisis. I had been a high school athlete, competing in nearly every sport imaginable. One of them was the high jump, which required flinging my body over a bar and breaking my fall in a sand pit with my left knee, with the impact transferred to my hip. I practiced that hundreds, probably thousands, of times. The damage didn't appear until my mid-forties in, of all places, North Carolina.

Years ago, when I had arranged for my newly constructed beach cottage to be rented for the summer, my lazy contractor was dragging things out for maximum profit. Disgusted with progress and with major grading to be done, I spent one entire weekend moving sand all over the property. I awoke on the last day with an excruciating pain in my hip which my physician diagnosed as an acute arthritic inflammation. He started me on enteric aspirin, which did little, and then put me on a stronger prescription pain reliever. It got me through the worst of times, but occasionally the pain was so severe I used a cane.

A few years after I moved to North Carolina, the pain became so intense I reluctantly went to an orthopedic surgeon to determine whether hip replacement surgery was needed. He said that I still had a little cartilage left and that I should delay surgery as long as possible, and he started me on a series of pain-relieving NSAIDS (nonsteroidal anti-inflammatory drugs).

Every single one of the over-the-counter and prescription NSAIDS tore up my GI tract. One of them even gave me a bleeding

## HISTORY OF MEDICINE

Outspoken Dr. William Douglass II offers a very interesting, very succinct history of medicine in his newsletter:

2000 B.C.: *Here, eat this root.*
1000 A.D.: *That root is heathen. Say this prayer.*
1850 A.D.: *That prayer is pure superstition. Here, drink this potion.*
1940 A.D.: *That potion is snake oil. Here, swallow this pill.*
1985 A.D.: *That pill is ineffective. Here, take this antibiotic.*
2003 A.D.: *That antibiotic doesn't work anymore. Here, eat this root.*

*Real Health*, June 2003, p. 3

intestine. When the last one failed, the surgeon told me to tolerate the pain as long as possible, and then come in for hip replacement. I was on my own. I stood outside his office and wondered why I should pay a princely sum for service worse than ineffectual. Since modern medicine couldn't help me, I decided to treat myself. I read everything in sight. One line of thinking in alternative medicine particularly appealed to me: since the ever-aging body produces less and less of the two principal building blocks of cartilage, nutritional supplements containing them might delay or even reverse the progression of osteoarthritis. I found those supplements at the nation's leading health emporium—WalMart—and started taking them at one-twelfth the daily cost of the prescription drug that gave me a bleeding intestine. After about a month, with no side reactions, I experienced a feeling of triumph when the pain began to subside. As I continued to read, I found reference to a naturally occurring anti-inflammatory that all humans regularly ingest in food, although in quantities too minute to treat arthritis. I began taking a supplement of that, too, and in just three days experienced a significant pain reduction.

That was six years ago. My hip is in better shape than it's been in twenty years and I don't intend ever to undergo hip replacement surgery. There I was, a man with a doctorate in public health from Johns Hopkins University, rejecting high-cost, ineffectual modern medicine for a few low-cost capsules per day that I could buy at WalMart—and with no side effects! The whole experience made me question the value of some things I had spent years learning.

Cleo, meanwhile, became ever more sedentary. There were more mornings when she didn't rush downstairs for the ride as well as the occasional mornings when she failed to come down at all, forfeiting the ride altogether. And she seemed to be having more difficulty negotiating stairs.

It was only then that I finally, finally recognized my stupidity. Cleo had arthritis like me!

After the vet confirmed the diagnosis, we asked if my anti-inflammatory supplement might help and she replied, "Probably." (I almost suggested she offer in-service training for physicians in the area.)

Well, we began inserting capsules in Cleo's food and, lo and behold, her mobility noticeably improved. What a great feeling! Cleo had the same problem I had and my do-it-yourself cure also helped her. I had bought some quality time for Cleo and me.

## DOGS AND HUMANS ARE SIMILAR GENETICALLY AND MEDICALLY

Tim Friend reported in *USA Today* pioneering findings on dog's genetic makeup.

Man's best friend is genetically more similar to his master than anyone might have imagined.

Scientists at The Institute for Genomic Research . . . report in today's *Science* completion of a rough draft of the dog's "book of life" and find that 75% of its genes have equivalents in the human.

The dog genome will advance the understanding of human diseases. . . . Scientists use dogs as models for more than 350 human diseases. When dogs are sick, they often have the same symptoms as humans with diseases ranging from arthritis to tumors.

The project reveals . . . that strings of mysterious genetic code between genes are identical in humans, dogs, mice and rats. . . . These regions may . . . represent basic control mechanisms for life. The dog genome is smaller than that for humans—2.1 billion letters of coding to our 2.9 billion letters.

*USA Today,* 10/26/03, p. 3A

A man currently in my mid-sixties, I can remember when knowledge of genetics, as well as many other fields of study, hadn't even reached the horse and buggy stage. With some delight, therefore, I read summary articles in the millennium year 2000 that summarized the technological changes throughout the twentieth century, one-half of which I had memory of. One article on genetics in *Time* magazine particularly interested me.

At the beginning of the twentieth century, the now-common terms of DNA and RNA were not even a gleam in science's eye. Charles Darwin knew nothing of them nor did his many critics. But technological advances, especially after World War II, quickly elevated the micro-world of humans to a position of prominence. Tiny strands of matter in billions of tiny cells determined more of what makes us *us* than anyone had previously imagined. The implications of it all were mind-boggling.

The article compared human genes to those in other species. The incredible similarity between human and chimpanzee genes received its already well-publicized consideration. Beyond that, however, there were some startling statistics not known to the general public. For instance, seventy percent of the genes in the common earthworm have matches in the human genome. (We have many more genes, of course, but they *include* matches with earthworm genes.) That is, indeed, startling.

Combining all the findings, the author of the article concluded that all living things on earth are genetically related. And the author tied all the loose ends together in the concept of *unity of life*. We are all related. We have a common origin.

I found that to be a wonderfully beautiful concept. Unity of life. We're all survivors from a legion of millennia on this hunk of rock in our solar system. Why do so many people feel threatened by such a concept? I personally do not feel degraded by the idea that an earthworm and I share some of the same ancestral genes.

That identity was evident in Cleo's having the same problem with arthritis that I had and the same response to the same nutritional supplements. At a more complex level of thinking, our shared genes gave both of us the same type of drive to give and receive affection, which made a wonderful bond between species possible. Millions of canine and human pairs experience the same thing every year.

Biology in general and evolutionary biology in particular search for explanations of the *differences* between species. "Unity of life" accents the sameness. I think that's important. It gives me a clearer understanding of life.

Judy and I entered a period of years during which there were few highs and lows, just week after week of routine. The dogs played a different role in family life then than Cleo had played during my period of isolation in Maryland. They added stability to an already stable lifestyle and offered a predictably pleasant dimension to the daily experience.

Irrespective of whether they had had a good day or a bad day, we could always depend on a warm welcome on returning home. If we decided to take them with us somewhere, they were always happy to go. If we felt like showering some affection on them, they never refused it. They were always there for us, day after day after day.

We tend to take such predictability for granted, which leaves us unprepared for abrupt changes. We were, therefore, unprepared for the day we found the lump on Cindy's side. It was cancer.

Cleo and Cindy related to the veterinary center entirely differently. Cleo, as usual, liked everyone there. Although she would have preferred not to be boarded during our occasional family trips, the bustle of human activity there prevented the experience from being traumatic.

Cindy, on the other hand, disliked being away from us for any period of time whatsoever and warmed up to strangers very, very slowly. Given that, I felt a little like a traitor when I left her for her surgery. Even without the attendant pain, this would be a difficult experience for her.

Cindy handled the post-op pain better than we expected while we awaited word on the outcome. It was cautiously optimistic, but we knew the possibility of recurrence was considerable. We smothered her with tender loving care and kept a wary eye on her side.

Cleo, meanwhile, was creating problems for herself. She eventually figured out that the bitter taste in her meals came from the nutritional supplement capsules. No matter what we tried, she found the capsules and she refused food in which we had mixed the powder. She became proficient at spitting the capsule out if we forced it by hand. It just wasn't working.

Our vet told us there was a pill from the pharmaceutical industry that was highly effective at controlling painful inflammation. We decided to give it a try and gave her the first pill one morning. After a period of hours, Cleo began running round and round the house. Finally, she stopped dead in her tracks and stared straight ahead. She was *thinking*! The pain was gone! She couldn't believe it. She ran for joy and to make certain it was really true. She began behaving like she had years earlier. Knowing personally how painful arthritis can be, I almost cried in happiness for her.

Alas, relief lasted only a week. The telltale signs of a side reaction began to appear. I got on the Internet and discovered the new medication had already become famous for its side effects. More than that, there were many documented cases of death. We discontinued the drug. When the signs of painful arthritis reappeared, we tried a drastically reduced dosage of the medication. It seemed to provide a little relief and there were no *visible* side effects.

As the weeks passed, I was distracted from worrying about the condition of my two dogs. Judy had back problems that now were worsening, and it became apparent she would need lumbar decompression surgery. Although it wouldn't be life-threatening surgery, any spinal surgery is worth worrying about.

We scheduled the surgery for late January. Since the hospital was two hours away, I decided to board the dogs and stay at a motel near the hospital for the two or three days she would be there.

On the fateful afternoon, I put Cleo and Cindy in the car and started for the vet's. My mind was on Judy, not them. About halfway there, Cindy began to whine, then howl, then utter the most pitiful sounds of agony I had ever heard from a dog. Somehow she had figured out where I was taking her and Cleo. She moved around the van as if she wanted to escape, crying uncontrollably all the time.

Cleo seemed undisturbed by the entire thing. I took her in first and she was happy to see all the folks there. When I took Cindy in, she didn't resist being taken to the back by the attendant, but her stiff walk and the positions of her tail and ears told me every muscle in her body was rigid with fear. I can't describe how bad I felt as I turned to go.

Judy's surgery went well and the dogs were delighted to return home, but we were soon jolted by yet another problem. The vet found that Cleo's kidneys were beginning to fail.

Golden Retrievers average about a dozen years of life and Cleo was there. For the first time, I had to admit to myself that her health would be all downhill from then on. I found processing that thought exceptionally difficult. She had been a daily joy for a dozen years, which is one-third of my entire adult life. It was hard to visualize her not being with me.

More than that, I found it difficult to accept that I would probably have to put her down since it was likely that the alternative would be to let her linger in pain. Although all of us have occasional arguments and tiffs with our parents, spouses, kids and even our closest friends, my relationship with Cleo had never experienced a single spat of any kind. She had the sweetest, most loving disposition of any human or animal I have ever known. We have nice words for the procedure—putting her down, euthanizing her, putting her out of her misery—but they just mask the fact that I would arrange for this lovely dog to be killed. Yes, it would be painless, but there would be no way to warn her of it or to give her a farewell meaningful to her. I simply didn't want to think about this. I knew I grasped the reality of it all when I remembered something for the first time in decades. Soon after our much-loved first cat, Checkers, had died prematurely in an auto accident, I had difficulty remembering what she looked like. She was about two-thirds white with black patches irregularly spread over her head and trunk. It was the arrangement of those patches that gave her a unique, cute look, and I couldn't remember their locations.

It was disturbing to find I had so few memories of such a beloved pet. She had entertained us in so many ways I guess I thought I could never forget. But I did, and I'm the poorer for it. Our lives up to now are our memories, and I had taken such poor care of them that I can now enjoy only a few. I did keep a file of interesting and humorous things the kids said and did, and I enjoy that file immensely from time to time. I wish I had done the same with my pets.

It crossed my mind that I hadn't photographed Cleo for several years and that I had better do it while I had the chance. I didn't want a repeat of the Checkers experience.

The photos I took startled me. I had apparently been relating mostly to Cleo's personality, but the photos revealed her physical features. I hadn't realized how old and subdued she had come to look. If I hadn't already understood how near the end was, those photos made it quite obvious.

It wouldn't be long. I wanted that last period to be among the best for Cleo and me.

My mother once said that when an animal exudes affection toward you, it's awfully hard not to love back. (She disliked cats, but offered that wisdom when one of mine crawled on her lap and went to sleep.) Cleo proved that. She loved everybody, especially those who came to visit awhile. My sister-in-law gave us a thank-you gift after a week's stay—a pillow featuring a large head of a Golden. My grandson, at summer camp, painted a long-eared ceramic dog brown. The ears are a little fluffier than a Golden's and the brown is a smidgeon off a Golden's color, but I got the message.

Even Cleo's reputation made an indelible impression on people. My sister in Ohio had never met Cleo, but remembered her name and always asked about her when she called.

In spite of her partially uncontrolled arthritis and the daily IV for her kidneys, Cleo remained outgoing, caring, gentle, affectionate and oh! so pleasant to be around. As my mother said, it's difficult *not* to develop intense loyalty to such a being.

I'm certainly not alone. Stories are legion about heroic, mutual loyalty between man and dog. I happened on one of them by chance on the Internet while Cleo was in failing health. I regularly watch a bit of CNN's *American Morning* show during breakfast and enjoy anchor Jack Cafferty's humor and human interest stories. I missed his live coverage of one story, but later found it on CNN's website, cnn.com. It was about an old, graying Golden Retriever that saved a baby's life.

It was about 4:30 A.M. and the mother was in the kitchen and the father was in the shower. Bullet, their Golden Retriever, came running into the kitchen, barked incessantly and seemed to try to coax the mother into the hallway. He refused to "go outside."

Worried, the mother checked on her baby and found him gasping for breath and turning blue. When the EMS finally transported the infant to the hospital, they found he had double pneumonia and an undiagnosed heart defect.

The mother told Cafferty she believed Bullet had saved the baby's life. She said Bullet believed it was *his* baby because it belonged to her. He was protecting *his* baby.

Cafferty probed into the family's history with Bullet. He found that the dog had been diagnosed with liver cancer a few years earlier. The vets had told the woman that she faced a difficult decision. The dog was old and the surgery was expensive and risky, with no guarantee against recurrence.

"I didn't know what to do," she related. "I said he's been a part of my life for all these years and there's no way I was going just to let him go." So she borrowed $5,000 for the surgery, which proved successful.

Cafferty spoke: "I have got dogs and cats in my house. I've had them all my life. I have feelings for animals that exceed the ones I

This is my last photo of my little friend.

have for a lot of the people I've encountered along the way. A story like this just affirms that I'm right."

The photos on CNN's website showed a dog eerily similar to Cleo—graying at the snout, sleeping spread-eagled with his jaw on the floor. He was snoozing next to the baby with the sleeping infant's hand on his side. In short, the family had a clone of Cleo.

The problem with this otherwise inspiring account is what Paul Harvey calls "the rest of the story." Sooner or later, Bullet's condition will deteriorate to such a degree that the family will face yet another gut-wrenching decision. Is the continuation of treatment, irrespective of cost, in the best interest of dog or family? Given Bullet's heroic, life-saving performance, the temptation obviously is to give him as long a life as possible. But at some point, Bullet's capacity to enjoy life will become dwarfed by his pain. The agony for the family to decide either way will be, or already has been, unspeakably excruciating.

We were faced with that type of decision soon after I found Cafferty's story. The cancer on Cleo's lip reappeared. Although one more surgery might be effective, the vet said her kidney condition was terminal. The arthritis, of course, would only get worse. Just how much longer could Cleo continue to enjoy life?

The answer came when Cleo's cancerous lip blistered badly and was obviously painful for her. We couldn't be selfish any longer. We had to let her go. We decided to enjoy Cleo's company one last weekend and scheduled the "appointment" for late Monday morning.

I have virtually no recollection of enjoying Cleo that weekend, but I vividly recall the unprecedented strain on Judy. She is a member of a church choir that requires her to practice before Sunday service and before I arrive with Kathy. When I did arrive, the choirmaster came to me and said Judy needed me. The stress of Cleo's impending death had overwhelmed her. She had broken down in tears. We decided to go home quietly.

We've taken our fair share of emotional "hits" in our years together, but that was the worst. I can't put it any plainer than that. We just plain hurt.

# The Worst Day Ever

Simple arithmetic revealed that I had taken Cleo on morning rides well over 4,000 times. They were as much a part of the morning as breakfast, shaving and reading the paper, but a whole lot more enjoyable.

Except for the last one.

Thankfully, Cleo didn't have to be teased downstairs and to the van. She snoozed now and then during the ride, poking her head up occasionally to see where she was. I must have looked back at her dozens of times to savor the last ride. I felt numb all over and resisted the temptation to take a longer ride than usual. When we arrived back home, she didn't come to my car door for attention but, as normal, she did exit the van before Cindy; I began to choke as I realized the last ride was over.

I suppose Judy made breakfast; I don't really remember. Our minds were on the first important chore of the day—digging the grave. We chose a shaded spot between two pine trees. I dug a very deep hole so that nothing would disturb my sleeping beauty. I recall being surprised there were no roots to cut through.

It was time to go.

I don't remember Judy or myself saying anything on the way to the vet's. Cleo entered the building without hesitation and seemed happy to see all the folks there.

I entered the examining room first. There was a diagonal bench in one corner on which I sat and to which Cleo came immediately, burying her head in my lap. She liked the people there, but her memories of that room weren't the fondest. I placed my hands under her ears and caressed her head gently. Since Cleo was so large, the vet said she would perform the euthanasia on the floor. Judy lowered herself to it and Cleo turned around and buried her head in Judy's hands while I scratched her backside. So help me, I think she understood that something terrible was about to happen to her and she trusted us to protect her.

The vet sheared off some hair from one paw. Cleo flinched ever so slightly, but didn't resist. She kept her head in Judy's hands and I scratched her back. As the vet slowly injected the fluid, Cleo didn't move a muscle—she died sometime during the procedure. It was over. My little girl was dead. Judy withdrew her hands from under Cleo's head and petted her one last time. I continued sitting there, shaking so badly I was afraid to try to stand.

Then came the most difficult part of all. The vet asked us to leave so they could wrap the body and take it to the car. I hadn't anticipated this; I had planned on having one last private moment with my little girl at our home before I buried her. I wanted to gaze at her one last time in private. But it was not to be.

I moved to where I could get a frontal view of Cleo, bending down to savor every part of her. I deliberately decided to stare as long as I needed to assure myself that I could remember her forever. I wanted to remember every detail.

She was spread-eagled as usual. Her head rested between her paws in her usual sleep position, eyes closed as in sleep. Her snout seemed grayer than usual. Her ears stretched motionless to the floor. The scene *in toto* was that of a peaceful, finally painless, sleep. God, she was beautiful.

I stared so long I could feel the vet moving nervously beside me. Assured that I had memorized every detail, I stood up and walked out. I had seen the last of my gentle little girl.

The ride home was as silent as the ride in. We carried the wrapped body to the gravesite and gently lowered her in. We said some words—I don't remember them. Then we stood there silently until there seemed no further reason to delay. As one last gesture of love, I placed a new tennis ball beside her.

Then I covered her up.

# Recovery and Reorientation

I've always been amazed at how quickly I've adjusted to the deaths of beloved pets. The day of their demise has always been devastating, but the routines of life have quickly recaptured my attention. I was grateful for that, but also puzzled by how quickly it took place.

It didn't happen with Cleo. Expectedly, after we buried her I spent the rest of the day in my study going through an entire box of facial tissues. After walking around for two weeks in a mental fog, I began feeling downright guilty about, and embarrassed by, my prolonged mourning period. I had always thought some dog owners went too far in their dog devotion. They dressed them in snazzy outfits and had their hair sheared into weird shapes and bought them super-expensive toys. After death, some paid small fortunes to have their pets mummified. Had I now joined the ranks of the extremists?

Everything about those two weeks reminded me of Cleo. The morning after, her water bowl at the bottom of the stairs didn't need filling and the ride with only Cindy was far less than enjoyable, to say the least. Judy brought me a swatch of Cleo's hair—something that I never thought to get before her death. When I took it to have it laminated, the young man there asked what it was; when I told him, he treated me to his own sorrowful history with dogs. I received e-mails from my two kids offering condolences. Judy received a sympathy card from a couple in the church choir who had also lost a beloved pet. My mentally challenged daughter kept asking where Cleo was.

That was the first week. When I went to church at the end of it, the woman who usually sat behind me asked where I had been the previous Sunday. When I explained about Judy, she nodded her head understandingly. She also had experienced painful losses. "Where else," she asked somberly, "can you slap somebody on the rump and then have your hand licked?"

My two grandkids from Maryland came to visit the second week. Shannon, only three, asked where "the other dog" was.

A visit to my photo shop proved to be the most interesting encounter that week. As I walked toward the store, I saw a car in the fire lane in front of it. A Golden Retriever was in the back seat, looking worriedly into the shop. He was a beautiful young adult. Although he tolerated my attention gracefully, he really wanted his master to hurry up and return to the car.

Inside, I engaged the master in conversation about Goldens. Turned out hers also feared loud noises like firecrackers and thunder. The busy shop owner didn't try to hurry either me or the master. When he got the chance, he told us all about his six dogs that he obviously loved deeply.

## MOURNING

One of the better collections of dog tales is *Best Dog Stories*, edited by Leslie O'Mara (Wing Books, 1990). The impressive list of authors includes the likes of O'Henry, James Herriot, Jack London, Albert Terhune and G. K. Chesterton.

The stories in the collection describe all sorts of human/dog relationships—some humorous, some inspiring, some wistful. But not one of them considers the mourning anguish of the owners after a pet's death or how they handled a loss. That type of silence may contribute to the unexpectedly devastating feeling so many people experience following a loss.

To obtain some idea of what people think and do about the mourning process, try the web search, "dogs AND mourning"—without the quotation marks. The websites you find may be informative and helpful.

Then I told the bank clerk about my loss of Cleo. She said her family dog, a mixed breed, died ten years ago. From that time to this, neither her kids nor her husband have allowed her to obtain another dog. They refuse to face the pain of another loss like that.

I was beginning to conclude that seemingly *everybody* out there loved dogs. Everybody was interested in them. Most had experienced a painful loss. Many owned one or more at that time. Clearly the reputation of "man's best friend" was accepted more widely than I had ever thought.

I knew when Cleo was alive that we shared a special relationship, but it was the intensity of my emotional devastation after her death that taught me just how special it had been. I wonder how many of those who shared their painful losses with me also had fully appreciated the depths of their attachments only after their pets died. I hope my readers with living dogs don't wait for a similarly devastating experience to become aware of just how much their pets mean to them.

In one of my more facetious moments, I wondered why we don't have a national "I Love Dogs" day. People could wear an "I Love Dogs" button so that dog lovers could make contact with each other. I don't know whether my barber or dentist or pastor or mailman love dogs. There are people I see frequently at the gas station, supermarket, convenience store and other places who might love dogs as much as I. A national day would help us locate each other and would add a different dimension to our relationships. We might all become a little more cordial to each other. Maybe it's not such a facetious idea after all. There's no reason we shouldn't relate to each other with as much consideration as we give our dogs.

Emotional ups and downs filled those first two weeks. Periodically I would close my eyes to assure myself I could still see Cleo on the vet's floor. I could, and I choked each time. I had never before experienced such an intense, prolonged emotional reaction.

During those first two weeks, I was much preoccupied with memory. My relationship with Cleo had been so meaningful that I refused to let it go, and the only way to hang on was with memory. But I hadn't foreseen the emotional drain of hanging on. Every time

I closed my eyes to recapture my last sight of Cleo, it hurt. That couldn't go on. It *shouldn't* go on.

There seems to be a consensus among professionals and lay persons alike that, although a mourning period for a significant loss is both natural and beneficial, it's important to get past it ASAP and get on with life. Otherwise several unfortunate consequences can occur: You may actually condition yourself permanently to associate the lost "person" with grief so that any recollection will be painful. Or you might join the ranks of those who live so much in the past that meaningful life today is sacrificed. This is particularly true of many elderly persons obsessed with either the good old days or the painful past. Life should be lived meaningfully *now*, the experts say.

Although there's much wisdom in this consensus, only one part of it applied to me. I didn't want my memory of Cleo to become permanently painful, and it might if I didn't shake the doldrums quickly. The rest of the consensus was either irrelevant to me or, in my view, completely wrong.

First of all, I think it gives the elderly a bum rap by focusing on symptoms rather than causes. Too many old folks have too much time on their hands and the easiest solution available to them is to sit around and rummage through their memories. Time management for the young consists of getting the most done in the least time so that their whirling-dervish lifestyles don't overwhelm them. For too many elderly, time management consists of finding enough meaningful things to do to make the day worthwhile. If they can't, they may unconsciously choose to live in the past.

Fortunately, Judy and I don't have that problem. We're as busy now as we were before retirement. Our main concern is finding the time to do all the things we want in the roughly twenty years we hope remain for us. And, even in my mourning period, I spent less time thinking about Cleo than I had spent with her when she was alive.

In addition to the bum rap for the elderly, I think the consensus completely misunderstands the importance of memory to people of all ages and the vital role it plays in living meaningfully *now*. Think of all the things people do to build a memory for the future. There's no other reason for taking photographs or keeping a diary or saving the kids' artwork or framing diplomas or keeping mementos or bronzing an infant's shoes or saving correspondence. Without really thinking about it, people go to great lengths to assure they won't forget some important experiences in their lives. Having done so, why should moderate "living in the past" be a bad thing? Living meaningfully *now* should include savoring the better experiences of the other ninety-nine percent of our lives—the past. After all, that's what we planned to do when we were having those experiences. And think of how often people *do* access their memory banks very deliberately. At family reunions, past experiences are freely and joyfully shared by all. At school reunions, the same. The family photo album is so important that people facing natural disasters often say they would save it first. People thoroughly enjoy returning to former neighborhoods, places of employment and those other "special" places like the place they got engaged. Even visiting gravesites can be a positive experience.

If we think about it—and most people don't—we go to great lengths to build a memory bank for the future and, when the future is *now*, we access it as a meaningful component of the day.

Millions of people consider their relationships with their pets to be, or to have been, such a valued part of life that they want their pets in their memory banks. They want them there joyfully instead of tearfully, and they want them there without being obsessed with them. *That* was what I concluded I wanted, but I wasn't sure how to do it. But I resolved to try.

Meanwhile, I had another great dog to occupy my attention—Cindy. It was very difficult to assess her reaction to Cleo's disappearance. She did seem to lie around more and to sleep more. It was she who had reached out to Cleo more than *vice versa*, so she must have missed her friend terribly.

Yet, she never passed up the opportunity to fill Cleo's shoes. As I had mentioned earlier, before leaving the van at the end of the morning ride, Cleo would stick her head out of my opened door to get some affection. Toward the end, it became too much effort on some mornings, so Cindy decided to pinch-hit for her. Although she enjoyed the attention, Cindy thought her primary responsibility was to survey the yard on my side of the van to make sure it was safe. She would look left, right, up and down before retracting her head. If she saw *anything* unusual at all, she'd give a whoop and holler and continue bad-mouthing the intruder—real or imagined—until the coast was clear. With Cleo gone, Cindy now made this her daily job and it worked—I never once was attacked by anything at the end of the morning ride!

But Cindy also assumed some of Cleo's other routines. You will remember that, after the morning ride, Cleo used to precede me up the stairs, stopping halfway up and turning so that I could reach down and give her a huge hug and a tummy rub. Lordy, how she loved to be hugged on those stairs. Again with Cleo gone, Cindy, who formerly trailed us up the stairs, moved up to beside me and stopped halfway up for attention. Instead of being hugged, she preferred to have me reach around and scratch her tummy. Oh, that felt so good she frequently stopped two or three times on the way up.

When it came to eating, Cindy could only partially fill Cleo's shoes. Cleo, you will recall, was ready to eat anything, anywhere, anytime, so she was always at the dinner table, patiently waiting for a few morsels. Cindy, as you also will recall, was finicky; sometimes she came and sat next to Cleo for morsels, but mostly not. There was never any competition between them. If I gave one a morsel, the other would wait patiently, knowing her time was coming. Their acceptance of each other and their trust in me truly amazed me.

With Cleo gone, Cindy became a regular at the table in her place. She would sit patiently beside me, assured I would eventually give her something. When I did, she would chew it and sort of stare at me, eye to eye, in a way I find difficult to express. Everything about her seemed totally relaxed, with her ears partially back and a soft, glazed look to her eyes like a child daydreaming. I came to enjoy watching her at such times so much that I gave her my last bite-size morsels no matter how hungry I was. She could be so incredibly gentle one moment, then transform instantly into a roaring monster at the first sound of the Hated Chevy. For some reason, I found her highly expressive mood swings extremely entertaining. She was a character, she was. And still is.

And, of course, I needed no alarm clock with Cindy around. When she thought it was time for me to get up, she would come to fetch me. If I was sleeping on my right side with my face inches from the bed's edge, she would position herself opposite my face and *breathe* on me. Now, it's not fair to say Cindy had bad breath, but it did have a "distinctive" aroma that made exiting slumberland desirable. If, on the other hand, I was sleeping on my left side, she would jump onto the bed and stomp around to find my legs before lying down.

Either way, I got up.

I relished my little friend's multi-faceted personality for a number of reasons. First, it was impossible to ignore her. Her personality features were highly visible at all times and she was always nearby. The show she put on all day long was great fun to watch. She was, indeed, a character. In fact, her personality was so overwhelming that I kept forgetting she was also the most beautiful dog I ever owned.

More importantly, she was in good health and I had learned from Cleo to enjoy that while I could because it wouldn't last forever.

And somewhat painfully, I knew Cindy might be my last dog. If I brought in another one now and he lived twelve to fourteen years, I'd be pushing eighty. Although I come from a family of long livers, there's no guarantee I won't be an exception and there's no guarantee that my health will remain strong enough to stay out of assisted living. If the new dog needed as much attention and restraint as Cindy, my kids couldn't handle her. Considering the degree to which Cindy clings to us, sending a similar dog away would traumatize her as much as it would hurt us. So I wasn't at all sure having one more dog would be in anyone's best interest. It wasn't the most pleasurable conclusion I ever reached.

During this period of reorientation after Cleo's death and my heightened appreciation of Cindy, I found myself super-sensitized to anything I saw in my community or in the media that had anything to do with dogs, animals in general, genetic research and a whole host of related topics.

There was a short piece on the evening news featuring a story of a dog rescuing a boy in the ocean. A black Lab jumped into the surf, swam to the boy, grabbed him by the collar of the life jacket he was wearing and dragged him to shore. The boy, however, was not in trouble in the water and definitely didn't want to be "rescued." The dog not only dragged him to the shoreline but all the way out out of the water. After he finally released the boy, he wagged his tail furiously as he awaited congratulations for his heroic deed. He seemed

## AN IRAQI DOG

I have a bad habit of putting *really* interesting material in a special place so it won't be lost, then forgetting where the special place is. That happened once again in the spring of 2003 after the Iraqi war began. Here is my best recollection of a fascinating newspaper account.

After the initial phase of the Iraqi War, a GI stationed in northern Iraq thought a dog might help with his sentinel duties. He asked the locals if they would find a dog for him, which they did—sort of. The newspaper account provided two photos. The first one showed a truly magnificent head of a light-colored German Shepherd. The second showed a skinny, emaciated body that suggested years of malnourishment and possibly much worse. One wonders whether the locals just dropped off a nuisance wretch that hung around the dumps for scraps of garbage.

By and by, the GI was ordered back to the States. Since he and the dog had become such close friends, he requested permission to take the dog back with him. Permission was denied for all the usual immigration and other bureaucratic reasons.

Back in the States, however, the GI missed the dog so much he began seeking waivers in the high echelons of the military, in Congress and in some private advocacy organizations. He received a great deal of sympathy, but no one knew how to work around the rules. Finally, however, an unnamed genius determined the dog could come here if he was made a war hero. It was done, and the animal jubilantly rejoined his grateful master in North Carolina.

The GI's wife said the dog lives solely for his master. He literally jumped for joy once when the GI emerged from a building while the wife was waiting with the dog outside. No quotes from the GI revealed the depth of his feelings for the dog, but his actions to retrieve the animal speak louder than words. He unquestionably did some jumping himself.

(continued on next page)

This is just one more story of the intensely close relationship dog and humans can form. There are countless accounts of dogs that have protected masters from attack, roused them from sleep at the first sign of fire, traveled long distances to find masters who moved and even, incredibly, barked to alert epileptic masters of an impending seizure. And, of course, the commitment from many humans is mutual.

Not all human/dog relationships are that special and most special relationships are not that spectacular, but I've found over the past years that those special relationships occur much, much more frequently than I had ever imagined.

very proud of himself. The boy just continued to lie there in a state of total disbelief about his rescue.

I found that little incident highly amusing and jotted it down lest I forget it. And I began cutting out interesting stories in the paper. I also began jotting down some occasional recollections of the good days with Cleo and my life with Cindy. It was fun to do and my pile of jottings and clippings grew and grew and grew.

It was amazing to find so much interesting material each week. It had been there all along, I guess, and I did pay attention to it if I had the time. With heightened awareness, however, I *made* time to savor each tidbit of information, every recollection and each appealing story.

One of the more interesting additions to my pile was a newspaper article four months after Cleo's death. It summarized the findings of three research papers on dogs in the November 22, 2002 issue of the popular journal, *Science*. I made a note of it and obtained the articles some time later.

The first article by Swedish scientist Peter Savolainen and associates reported on a study to locate the geographic origins of domesticated dogs and to estimate the date of domestication. The researchers studied the DNA of "654 domestic dogs representing all major dog

## MITOCHONDRIAL DNA

Think of the cells in your body as chicken eggs, although much smaller. In each cell (egg) there is a large nucleus (yolk) surrounded by fluid inside the cell membrane (shell). Most of your genetic material in each cell is in the nucleus and comes equally from your mother and father. It is very difficult to trace your genetic ancestry very far back in time using nuclear DNA.

In the fluid surrounding the nucleus, however, there is genetic material (DNA) in long, skinny strands called mitochondria. That genetic material comes only from your mother and is an exact duplicate of hers. Because of that, researchers are able to use it to trace genetic ancestry back thousands of years. A very understandable explanation of the methodology for doing so is found in pioneering researcher Bryan Sykes' bestseller, *The Seven Daughters of Eve* (Norton, 2001). Using this new methodology, Sykes found that most of Europe's current human population traces back to seven female immigrants. Since dogs' cells also contain mitochodrial DNA, the same methodology can be used to trace their origins.

populations worldwide." The research employed a relatively new methodology involving mitochondrial DNA.

They found that all domestic dogs today are descended from the same gene pool in East Asia, which dates back about 15,000 years ago. Those earliest domesticated dogs were genetic descendants of about a half-dozen female wolves.

The second article agrees with the first in regard to American dogs that were here long before Columbus and subsequent colonization. Using the same mitochondrial DNA methodology, UCLA researcher Jennifer Leonard and associates found that "mitochondrial DNA sequences isolated from ancient dog remains from Latin America and Alaska show that native American dogs [were descended from the

Eurasian dogs] that accompanied late Pleistocene humans across the Bering Strait [to North America]."

The third article switches gears to a more tightly focused study using a different methodology. Harvard anthropologist Brian Hare and associates report their findings in the published abstract in *Science* (11/22/02):

Dogs are more skillful than great apes at a number of tasks in which they must read human communicative signals indicating the location of hidden food. In this study, we found that wolves that were raised by humans do not show these same skills, whereas domestic dog puppies only a few weeks old, even those that have had little human contact, do show these skills. These findings suggest that during the process of domestication, dogs have been selected for a set of social-cognitive abilities that enable them to communicate with humans in unique ways.

Archeological findings are consistent with the dates from mitochondrial DNA research and suggest that the newly domesticated dog spread nearly worldwide in an amazingly short time. The oldest unearthed dog remains in Israel, Iraq and Germany date back about 13,000 years. The oldest remains in North America in Utah's Danger Cave date back about 10,000 years. Indeed, migrating populations and traders took their precious canines with them everywhere they went. Although neither DNA nor archeological research can document an affectionate bond between man and dog, the dig in Israel strongly suggests one. The human skeleton unearthed there cradled a puppy skeleton in its left hand.

Adding other findings, some common sense and a little imagination to these three studies allows us to make an educated guess about the domestication process.

The story begins with the gray wolf, which is found worldwide in the Northern Hemisphere. It was, and still is, an intelligent, highly social animal that lived and hunted in packs with social stability maintained by a dominant wolf or male/female pair. They were, and are, great team players.

Especially during times when food was scarce, those wolves with the least fear of humans probably frequented human settlements in search of some discarded morsels. Puppies from deceased or abandoning females near the settlements were likely cared for by the humans, as they still are. Some of those puppies with the most compatibility with humans stayed at or near the settlements and reproduced. Others that didn't "fit in" either left or were killed or sometimes eaten. Over many canine generations, the settlement animals became more and more like the animals the humans wanted them to be.

Being social animals and having a need to obey a leader gave the slowly changing wolves a leg up, so to speak, on domestication. At some point, the changing animals were able to transfer their need to obey to a human leader. At that point, the dogs became useful as hunting partners and probably protectors against predators. After cattle, goats and sheep were domesticated beginning about 10,000 years ago, dogs became useful as herders of the very animals their ancestors preyed on. Since the horse was domesticated much later, the dog served as a beast of burden for millennia.

Being both social and obedient by heritage produced a new animal that was both useful to and companionable with humans. No other animal species in human history has combined the traits of usefulness and companionability as well as the dog. It is little wonder then that these precious animals were welcomed by human communities all over the world. Dogs didn't become man's best friend by Darwinian natural selection, but by human selection. We have deliberately transformed the dog into what he is today and, for a change, we did something right. Although chimpanzees are our closest genetic relative and have an overall intelligence superior to dogs, our canine friends have been tailor-made by us for intimate contact in human society.

After the still incompletely understood domestication of dogs and their distribution over a large part of the ancient world, selective breeding began and has continued to this day. Literally hundreds of different breeds have been recognized for their distinctive physical and behavioral traits.

Although companionability has become increasingly valued in recent times, dogs are still useful in hunting, herding and protection as well as in many ways not imagined even a hundred years ago. They are only recently useful as wartime sentinels and messengers, law enforcement helpers (e.g., sniffing out narcotics), service dogs (e.g., for the blind), cartoon entertainers (e.g., Snoopy and Howard Huge), movie stars (from the elegant Lassie to the slobbering comic in *Turner and Hooch*) and therapists for the chronically ill, institutionalized elderly and shut-ins. Their proven usefulness in medical research has generated considerable controversy. No other animal has been as useful to humans in as many ways as the dog; no other animal is close enough even to deserve second place.

Although the *number* of uses for dogs has expanded, the majority of dogs in modern society are owned for companionship, purebreds and "hybreds" alike. Many young parents get a dog for the kids because that's just part of family life, isn't it? Single or widowed persons living alone can become desperate for a living thing to love. There's something about puppies that makes persons of all ages and life circumstances want to pick them up and cuddle them. Countless times I've watched as toddlers see a dog and instantly gravitate toward him. Our positive predisposition toward dogs is so strong that we cringe when we hear of neglect or abuse, and we tend to write off dog attacks as exceptions worth forgetting. We made the dogs the way we wanted them, so it's no surprise so many of us want them just because they are dogs.

Most people don't think of their canine pets in this larger historical and contemporary context. I didn't until two exceptional relationships got me thinking about why they became so important to me. The larger context helped me get over my agonizing sense of loss over Cleo. It helped me appreciate Cindy more and prepare a positive memory of her. The little exercise of notes and clippings I started after Cleo's death took minimal time and considerably expanded my understanding of myself, the living world I'm part of, the nature of man/animal relationships and how human society got to its present status in the living world. I decided to continue my little exercise until it ceased to be meaningful.

# Understanding It All

Never before had I spent time trying to understand my memory. What is it? How does it work? What are its uses? How can I manage it? The answers to these questions are obviously important, but you probably don't have them and neither did I. Most of us haven't addressed such questions since our school days when we tried little memorization tricks in preparation for exams.

I decided to try a little experiment to shed some light on the subject. I asked myself what family event in the past was my most cherished memory, and the answer came instantly. It was a thirty-day camping tour of the parks and wildlife preserves in the West. I had bought a pop-up camper and all five of us climbed into our full-size van for our most ambitious adventure together. It was the best single time we ever had as a family and I was positive my memory banks were full to overflowing. I knew that past event was memorable for the sheer quantity of pleasurable little experiences, in contrast to a single event like buying my first car.

That morning, when the Sunday paper failed to arrive on time, I sat down and listed as many of the trip's experiences as came to mind easily. There was the first herd of bison I had ever seen and the spectacular view from a Colorado mountaintop. The goats in Montana's Glacier National Park were fascinating, especially when a new mother descended out of the mist with her little one trudging behind. By the time my memory began to stall, I had a list of eleven memorable experiences.

Eleven? Surely there were more than that! After church, therefore, I sat down and fifteen more came to mind quickly. There were the incredibly pleasant people at Mount Rushmore who impressed us greatly and the numerous bald eagles along the Snake River and more.

These brought the list to twenty-six, but still that's less than one per day. There had to be more than that!

The next evening, I sat down and retraced our meanderings through eleven western states. When I had finished, I had seventy-eight experiences. There were the friendly ground squirrels in Montana and the splashes of color in the Painted Desert. At the cleanest campgrounds I've ever seen, my son and I marveled that the owners even placed potted geraniums in the restroom.

I knew that spending more time would yield even more memories of experiences that, at the time I had them, I hoped to retain in my memory. But I had enough to start drawing some conclusions.

Most of the time when Judy and I and the kids refer to the trip, it's a quick "that was the best trip we ever took" comment, usually followed by one or two shared experiences. Clearly when the mind recalls in a short time a long set of experiences, it abstracts to a general attitude toward the set as a whole. "Wow, that was *some* trip." And we get used to flashing one or two favorite images through our consciousness in support of that. Those favorite experiences were in my first set of eleven.

In the second set of fifteen, most items in the list were infrequently recalled experiences. And I couldn't recall ever thinking about most of the experiences in the third set; they came to mind only when I sat down and carefully retraced our steps. Although we took a slew of slides, there are things that cannot be photographed and they tended to show up in the third set. For instance, as I retraced our steps, it struck me that things that hadn't happened contributed enormously to the trip's success. The van didn't act up; the camper gave us no problems; no one became ill or injured. Those types of non-happenings are worth remembering, too, even though they can't be photographed.

In principle, recalling life with Cleo was like recalling the trip. It was the sheer number of wonderful experiences over a long time that made our relationship memorable. Yes, I had a few favorite experiences that readily came to mind when I thought, and still think, about her. But what else had I relegated to some dusty storage bins in my mind?

Almost instantly I recalled when Judy took Cleo to visit the patients in the local nursing home. It was managed by a friend of ours and followed the philosophy of the Eden Alternative, which strived to make nursing *homes* as homey as possible. That included having plants and pets all over the place. So Cleo was just as welcome there as any other visitor. Judy said she didn't know who had the better time, Cleo or the patients. Possibly I would have left that memory in a storage bin forever. It took an effort to recall it.

And I recalled the time I stopped to buy something at the Kitty Hawk Fishing Pier. About halfway up the ramp, I felt something brush against my leg. I looked down and saw Cleo beside me, moseying along matter-of-factly. Since I had left the car window completely open, my little girl decided to jump out and join me. Gee, I enjoy recalling that now. It reminds me that Cleo felt she should be with me at all times; if I left the window completely open, that meant she could join me if she wished, and she wished.

Re-invigorated by these findings, I continued to add to my pile of jottings, newspaper clippings and computer printouts. And, from time to time, I drew further conclusions from the experiment. For instance, it dawned on me that many of the recollections I've had about the trip occasionally were triggered by something unrelated to it. A magazine photo of the Grand Canyon, for instance, would call to mind the awed feeling I had when I was there. As such, those memories were *reactive* recollections. If I wanted to remember other experiences that weren't triggered by external stimuli, I would have to work at it. I would have to be *proactive* to use my memory the way I wanted.

An experience with Cindy provided an opportunity to do so. To become completely proactive, I would have to create my own memory stimuli now and deliberately activate it later. So I jotted down my little experience with Cindy right after it happened. Here it is just as I wrote it, with the English cleaned up a bit.

> I was working down in my study while Judy was at the store and Cindy was somewhere upstairs. I finished a project and took it out to my car lest I forget to take it with me later to the post office for postage. Cindy was on the porch and barked her willingness to ride with me. But when I just returned to the house, Cindy began crying in a way that told me she was lonesome. I whistled upstairs for her to come down if she wanted, but she just cried a little longer and stayed upstairs. That was unusual, but she could remain upstairs if she wanted.

Cindy's appearance has changed little over the years except for some graying of the snout. She's as energetic and playful as ever. Even with her ears back in the neutral position, she still has an alert look about her in this photo.

Half an hour later, I went upstairs and saw the problem. There's a sliding glass door leading to the porch which Judy had left partially open so Cindy could go in and out, but the opening was too small. Cleo, strong as she was, would have stuck her head through and opened the door. Cindy, however, considered all barriers inviolate, so she simply accepted being marooned out there.

Cindy was lying at the door, facing away from it. Quietly, I snuck up to the door and very slowly opened it another half-foot. She didn't hear me. I moved off about twenty-five feet and made a few little noises. Cindy stood and turned to see what was happening. She saw me, wagged her tail and waited for me to come and open the door for her, which I didn't do. Then she noticed that the door seemed open enough for her to pass through. That didn't seem right to her, so she studied it some more. Eventually she stuck her head through, then her front paws, wagged her tail and jumped all the way through.

She jogged right over to me to receive a congratulatory pat, but then backed off and gave me a loud, long piece of her mind. How dare I entomb her out there on the porch all by herself? I'm not sure, but she might also have figured out that I had pulled a trick on her.

At any rate, she was too happy to see me to stay angry long. She asked for more physical reassurance and followed me downstairs.

It wasn't a major experience, lasting perhaps four minutes, but it was one of those ever-so-frequent little happenings that make the total experience of loving a pet so memorable. Without jotting it down, I probably wouldn't have remembered it a week later.

I usually don't write out the whole experience, just a couple sentences as reminders. After reading the above narrative a month later, however, I enjoyed it so much I decided to do it more often.

I thoroughly enjoyed my little memory experiments. They taught me how to prepare and manage memory so that I can retrieve in the future the experiences of today that I want to keep in temporary storage. I will have an easier time remembering Cindy than I have had remembering Cleo.

We entered the twentieth century after millennia of believing that man was intrinsically superior to all other animals. To be sure, some animals were stronger than us or swifter or more capable of withstanding extremes of heat and cold. Some could see better or hear better or find their way more efficiently. But, although man did not top the list in many of these physical and behavioral attributes, we did outrank everything else in intelligence. That, in the minds of most, made us not only *superior* to animals but also fundamentally *different* from them. Indeed, there was widespread doubt that animals possessed any type of intelligence at all.

The sheer weight of scientific research over the past century has been revolutionizing our understanding of animals and their relationship to us. Studies of anatomy, physiology, genetics, behavior and more support each other in the emerging belief that there is a continuum of species within which *Homo sapiens* is only one member. Studies point to many gradations of intelligence in the animal world, a full complement of emotions like ours and a surprising amount of life-consciousness. There still is resistance to this new orientation in parts of the popular culture, in the religious community and even in some scientific quarters. Yet the ever-growing body of evidence for the unity of life is gradually shifting the net attitude in society from doubt to a welcoming attitude toward our recently recognized relatives. George Page wrote in *Inside the Animal Mind* (Broadway Books, 1999, p. xiii):

> Personally, I like very much the idea that my kinship with the other living creatures of the earth might be much greater than our scientific and cultural heritage has led us to believe. I am comfortable with the fact that, like them, I am an animal and that many of the characteristics that I have so often passed off as being "just a part of human nature" . . . may, in fact, be aspects of our shared animal natures.

## INSIDE THE ANIMAL MIND

Go to www.pbs.org and search for *Inside the Animal Mind*. There are three videos and a companion volume for sale at a reasonable price. You can buy the whole set or any one of the videos: (1) "Are Animals Intelligent?" (2) "Do Animals Have Emotions?" (3) "Animal Consciousness."

George Page is the creator and host of *Nature*, which has enjoyed two decades of unparalleled popularity with PBS. *Inside the Animal Mind* is the companion volume for three videos (same title) on animal intelligence, emotions and life-consciousness. The entire set is available from PBS (see sidebar) and offers the best, most understandable selection of studies I have found. Although it is not the intention of this book to offer a comprehensive review of animal (including human) research, the studies in the PBS series and Page's companion volume are a fascinating sample of the literature available. I offer only one example here. It deals with the highly complex and widely challenged notion of social consciousness in animals. That is, can an animal think about itself, simultaneously understand what another animal or human is thinking and link the two logically? Here is one study in brief that suggests an answer.

Visualize two small rooms separated by glass with a chimpanzee on one side and a trainer on the other. The trainer has two small, lockable boxes in front of him that the chimp can see plainly. The key to the locks is hung on a string a foot above the boxes, also visible to the chimp.

The trainer asks the chimp what kind of food she wants and she signals "apricot." The trainer produces one, places it in one of the boxes, locks the box and re-hangs the key—all in the chimp's field of view. Then the trainer leaves the room for a time, during which a different trainer enters. The chimp *seems* to understand that the second trainer doesn't know where the apricot is, so she points to the right box; the trainer then unlocks it and gives her the treat she wanted.

Then the experiment is repeated with an important twist. During the first trainer's absence, the second trainer enters the room and moves the key across the room. When the first trainer returns, the chimp points to the new location of the key. Then she points to the right box, which is unlocked and she receives her treat.

In one fell swoop, the chimp has demonstrated intelligence, the ability to send and receive communication, motivation for pleasure (emotion) and all types of consciousness.

## HARVARD LAW OF BIOLOGY

Indirect evidence for animal intelligence comes from the fact that animals do things their way, not ours. Murray Wylie, a Scottish physician, introduced me to the Harvard Law of Biology, which may or may not be apocryphal: "Under precisely controlled environmental conditions, experimental animals do whatever they damn well please."

"Social" consciousness is the highest form of consciousness. *The chimp knew that the second trainer didn't know where the key had been moved,* so she told him where it was. Stated differently, the chimp knew what she knew and knew what the trainer didn't know, so she communicated a solution to him. Similar experiments with other chimps have documented the same ability. But this type of inter-species, shared consciousness and communication is simply astounding!

Snakes cannot do what the chimp did, nor can mice, deer, skunks, blue jays or sharks. But they *can* do less complex tasks requiring a less fully developed form of the same intelligence and emotions we have. Literally thousands of studies have demonstrated that in every corner of the world.

Early researchers were much concerned with anthropomorphism, the tendency to see human characteristics in "lower" forms of life. That concern came from the long-held premise that humans are fundamentally different from animals. One hears less about anthropomorphism these days because anatomical, biochemical, physiological and genetic studies have demonstrated that "apparent" human characteristics in animals are, in most cases, real—just less complex. Interestingly, no one has coined a word for projecting superior animal abilities onto inferior humans in performance areas such as sight and hearing. Only humans are arrogant enough to base their claim to superiority on one parameter, intelligence, ignoring all others. (Actually, arrogance is a dimension of personality for which humans can claim complete superiority.)

If there's anything I've enjoyed doing throughout my entire life, it's photography, especially nature photography because it's a challenge. Birds and land animals aren't fond of posing and they usually won't let you near them, so I've accumulated lenses from 28 mm to 800 mm and just about every gadget the industry manufactures.

On the humble side, however, I've made the same mistake over and over, decade after decade. I frequently took my kids on expeditions and then photographed deer on the run, sunrises between downpours and waterfowl on the wing without taking a single shot of my kids, Judy or myself. I could always do that later, I told myself, and seldom did.

Cleo suffered the same fate. When I finally admitted to myself that she was dying, I went through my mounds of slides and prints.

It was a shock. I had very few photos of her, especially in her younger years, and those I did have were of the use-up-the-roll variety—very poor. Since I shoot virtually anything that moves, I know I took more shots than I've found. Some may been lost in my move to Carolina and others may still be buried in my super-voluminous, but poorly organized, files. Lordy, I hope so.

As an aid to memory, photos probably top the list in most homes. The family album provides moments of shared joy from time to time: "Wow, you look so young in that picture." Especially, photos of children and grandchildren grace our desks and walls, and some even survive years in our wallets under ever-increasing weight. If I can give one piece of advice to my readers, it is this: Take photos of your pets as often as possible. You won't get a second chance.

Yet photos aren't enough. They can't help me remember how it felt to run my fingers through Cleo's silky-soft fur. They can't help me recall her pitifully gentle *wooo-wooo* when the hated Chevy passed. I almost invariably didn't have my camera with me when memorable moments occurred, such as her jumping out of the car at the pier. They can't help me remember how I *felt* when I realized my little puppy was something special, or the many other times I felt so honored to have her. There's no alternative to putting pen to paper to record indelibly all those cherished moments and feelings that can't be photographed.

I've been jotting down recollections and cutting out stories for nearly a year now. The size of the pile is astounding, considering how little time I spend on it each day. A couple months ago, however, I realized that my collection was like having all the parts of an automobile in a pile in the driveway. It isn't a car until the parts are assembled. So I began sorting the individual entries chronologically from the time I first met Cleo.

I knew I needed more photos and I wasn't sure how many more would surface when I took the time to search my files. When I found someone online selling three books on Golden Retrievers, I thought I might find a few exact matches with Cleo's appearance, so I bought them. Incredibly, not a single photo was an exact match. None of them had eyes as soft as Cleo's and there was something gentle about Cleo's forehead that none of the dogs in the books had.

I finally hit pay dirt at WalMart. There was a collection of photo calendars, one of which was devoted solely to Goldens. One month's featured Golden was Cleo's double. I grabbed it before anyone else could.

I should have anticipated what happened next. When I presented the calendar to the woman at the checkout counter, she said, "That's my baby!"

"You have a Golden Retriever, too?" I asked.

"Yes, I love him to pieces."

From that time to this, I always get in that woman's line, even if it's a little longer than the others, and we exchange pleasantries about our dogs. It completely changes mundane visits to a store. It personalizes them. I have something in common with someone there, and I don't even know her name.

With time, I've found two more exact likenesses of Cleo and have taken the necessary steps to assure I won't encounter the same problem with Cindy some day. There are no others of Cindy's breed in the community, no calendars with them and no TV commercials featuring them; it will be much more difficult to protect my visual memory of her later, so I have to act now.

Please, folks, take photos of your pets regularly. You don't want your best shots to be those of the end. That's not how you want to remember your little friends.

I have included mostly upbeat topics in these pages, ranging from the affectionate bond between a single human and a dog all the way up to how we humans understand our relationships with the entire animal world. Reality, of course, is not always so upbeat. I have not, for instance, commented on the extensive abuse of pets, farm animals, experimental animals and wildlife. Those are important topics for others to develop in other types of books.

I have, however, commented earlier on the continuing hostility between some religious leaders and some scientists around the topic of evolution. Using myself as an example, I have stated that I consider the hostility unnecessary, that the two sides are not incompatible unless one chooses to make them so. And some people so choose. I was dismayed in my mourning period to find the battles raging just as fiercely as they were a century ago.

The most recent flare-up began shortly before Cleo's death. In the June 18, 2002 issue of *Scientific American,* editor John Rennie published an article entitled "15 Answers to Creationist Nonsense." The content matched the title exactly.

In the July 29, 2002 issue of *US News and World Report,* Thomas Hayden wrote the cover story on evolution; the generally dispassionate article, however, did take a few swipes at creationism. In a companion article, Holly Morris commented on the creationists' most recent strategy to weaken evolution in high school curricula. They advocate teaching ID (intelligent design) as an alternative to evolution. (ID holds that the various species could not have developed by random chance but, instead, by the intervention of an external, intelligent force. ID does not explicitly attribute the intervention to God, but . . . .)

Creationists, expectedly, saw red when these articles appeared. For a while, a vituperous back-and-forth debate ensued online, with creationists roasting evolution's knowledge base and evolutionists attacking the quality of their opponents' research and logic.

It's a free-for-all out there, folks, and we seem to be making little or no progress toward a homogeneous cultural understanding of the living world, its origins and the interrelationships among the species.

I would bet dollars to doughnuts that both creationists and evolutionists care for their pet dogs equally well in spite of their different definitions of what a dog is. Rover, fortunately, doesn't care what their beliefs are and the affection he expresses without reservation demands a return in kind. That seems to be the only thing the two sides have in common. Incredibly, Rover seems to have the best chance at this time of bridging the gaping chasm between the extremes. Well, no . . . that seems impossible even for Rover.

With all the attention to my memory of Cleo and some broader issues that surround the owner-pet relationship, has Cindy been ignored?

Far from it. First of all, it's impossible to ignore her. She's the most *involved* pet we've ever had. No motion, sound or odor escapes her attention. She believes she should be right in the middle of whatever's happening, and she is.

More than that, however, she's just fun to be around and watch. Except when she's sleeping, she's constantly looking around, visiting other rooms to check on things, watching us or the cats, barking at passing dogs or the Hated Chevy, seeking a little attention, enjoying a morsel or two, or generally occupying herself with one thing or another. And even more than that, she's a cute dog. For me, at least, she's charismatic.

She's also the most intelligent dog I've ever had. Recently while I was driving, Cindy sat on the rear platform, taking in the sights as usual. I enjoyed checking on her in my rearview mirror. While idling at a stoplight, I watched her savoring all the activity around us. Suddenly, she made eye contact with me through the rearview mirror and immediately came forward to get a little attention, wagging her tail furiously. Cindy has always been an eye-contact dog, reading my mood and my interest in her. If I perfunctorily pet her without making eye contact, she concludes I don't mean it and walks away.

Well, now that she's figured out how to make eye contact with me through the mirror, she uses it to check on me the same way I use it to check on her. None of my other pets ever learned to do that.

George Page made a comment in *Inside the Animal Mind* that intrigues me. He said science is still trying to prove things about animal capabilities that pet owners already know. That is, just because science has had difficulty *proving*, for instance, that some animals have human-like emotions doesn't mean they don't.

Cindy is a good example. She has a marvelous sense of time. If we are behind in our daily routines, she reminds us. And we're expected to come home at the regular time. One day, however, Judy was long overdue and Cindy became worried, as I was. When her car finally pulled into the driveway, Cindy let out one yipe, leaped into the house from the porch, ran round and round the living room, jumping for joy every ten feet, and returned to the porch to greet Judy with her tail in high gear. That's emotion.

Someday everybody will agree that many animals have human-like emotions. All they have to do is look.

# Into the Future

The first anniversary of Cleo's death came and went with remarkably little emotion. I visited her gravesite, of course, and did choke up a bit, but nothing close to my expectations. The efforts I'd been making to redirect my memory to the early, joyful days may have been working.

I was more preoccupied with another explanation, however. My memory of Cleo seemed to be fading. About a week earlier, I noticed that Cindy's tail seemed to be more curled than before and I wondered whether Cleo's tail position had also changed over her lifetime. But, strangely, I couldn't visualize what that position had been. After thinking about it for a few minutes, I concluded it was sort of straight back, but I wasn't sure until I checked one of her photos.

Additionally, when I visualized Cleo on the vet's floor as I had done dozens of times before, it seemed that some details of lesser importance were fading. That may have resulted from the gradually diminishing pain I felt during those recollections.

Even the laminated swatch of hair on my bulletin board had lost some luster.

If it is inevitable that I will lose some detailed recollections over time in spite of my efforts to hold on, which memories do I want to protect the most? I spent most of one Saturday morning on that question and isolated three highest priority memories.

Most of all, I want to remember Cleo for transforming one of the dreariest periods in my life into one of the happiest. I want to visualize myself and young Cleo whizzing around the Middle Atlantic states in our trusty truck with windows wide open, music blaring from four speakers and hot coffee for me and a shreddable cup for her. Lawd Ahlmighty, those were exhilarating times. Those were *special* times.

Next, I want to remember Cleo's middle years, during which nothing unusual happened. Day after day, Cleo was always there, always ready to go with me, always ready to give and receive affection. If you had to pay for an uplifting dimension to every single day for years with not one single exception, how much would you be willing to pay? That can't be bought, of course, but it sure is worth remembering, even though the memories satisfy less than the actual joyful experiences.

I hope my readers don't wait until their beloved pets die to appreciate the depth a human-animal relationship can reach. What a colossal shame it is to understand the possibility *after* the pet has died.

Finally, I want to remember the pain I felt during Cleo's decline and at her death. It is the measure of how much my little girl meant to me. No other loss of any kind has devastated me so much. We had an extraordinarily special relationship and its loss deserves an experience of pain simply because humans reserve that emotion for significant losses, and the loss was significant indeed.

## QUALITY = EXPERIENCE X 3

I've come to believe the definition of the *quality* of one's life *at any given moment* is the sum total of the memorable experiences to date, the experiences of the moment and the planned memorable experiences of the future. Inattention to any one of these three diminishes the net life experience. Obsession with the past has received, in my opinion, an inordinate amount of negative attention and ridicule. So has daydreaming about, but not planning for, the future. I now believe the most unfortunate souls on this planet are those so obsessed with responding to the demands of the moment that they neither savor the quality of the past nor work toward a memorable future. That's most of *Homo sapiens. (Sapiens?)* Thanks, Cleo, for teaching me that. And thanks, Cindy, for reinforcing it. Isn't it strange that I learned so much about the meaning of human life from another species?

Days later it dawned on me that all three of these memories focused on my *relationship* with Cleo over periods of time. That realization allowed me to feel better about the dearth of good photos of her. One cannot photograph a relationship or period of time and, anyway, it's rare that a camera is ever at hand when specific memorable events happen. Although photos are useful as reminders and as catalysts for memory, it's the day-in, day-out sharing of loyalty, affection and trust that's memorable, not a single episode.

Cleo's legacy to me contains three other important components, all related to general interests in life.

First, I hadn't spent much time in recent years on the creationism/evolution controversy until my grieving period exercises brought me up to date on some of the current gruesome twists in the debate. Although I'm religious, I once again felt discouraged that the religious far right still refused to acknowledge that science had contributed any insights at all over the two thousand years since the Bible's contents were finalized. (I recall with dismay a televangelist who shook a Bible at the camera and shouted, to the best of my recollection, "All we need to know is in here." He didn't acknowledge, of course, that his Bible and the TV camera were products of modern science.) And there's still a vocal minority of scientists who revel in their ridicule of "country bumpkin" religious conservatives. The current status of the debate is not something in which the species *Homo sapiens* can take much pride.

Additionally, my exhilarating relationship with Cleo energized my sometimes active, sometimes dormant interest in all living things. Without that revitalization, I might not have recognized the importance of the concept of "unity of life." That beautiful concept tied all sorts of loose ends together for me. (There are no loose ends in nature because all living things are part of the same design; there are only loose ends in how we understand it.)

Finally, of course, Cleo forced me to try to understand my memory and to appreciate its colossal importance. I had never before spent even a minute of my life wondering what memory was or how it can be both protected and controlled. Although these pages have focused mainly on two dogs, I have applied my newfound understanding of memory to the entirety of my life. For instance, we had to euthanize one of our cats shortly after the anniversary of Cleo's death. We had lived with her for over eighteen years and loved her dearly. I took one last photo of her and, upon returning from the

## INTELLIGENT MEMORY

The simple memory exercises described here understate modern technical understanding of memory and its management. Memory is no longer considered to be simply a matter of information storage and retrieval. It is now linked to most cerebral functions, conscious and unconscious, and management of it now includes dozens of techniques.

For a nontechnical discussion of broadly defined memory, see Dr. Barry Gordon's *Intelligent Memory* (Viking Penguin, 2003).

vet's, I wrote up how I wanted to remember her. I have also pulled out the jottings I made when the kids were growing up and started adding details before time wiped out any more of my memory. I now have a memory pile for everything I want to remember. I will sort it from time to time.

It amazes me that my memory pile has consumed so little time. Anything I want to remember about literally anything goes into the pile and it just takes a minute or two a day, on average. It's a little like the family photo album. We let the photos pile up, then sort and paste them in. The difference with my pile is that most of its contents are written notes, not photos. We can't capture *everything* on film. A memory pile seems at least as important as a family photo album. I wonder why I never thought of it earlier in life, an omission probably shared by most of my readers.

My story about Cleo and Cindy has been dominated by Cleo, by design. It was Cleo who taught me that man and "beast" could actually form a special relationship worthy of being called friendship. When I purchased her, I had a much lower expectation of our lives together; this expectation dramatically and quickly improved with time. Without my experience with Cleo, I might have related entirely differently to the terrified little creature Judy brought home from school. Although Cindy immediately reached out to me for protection and affection, I might just have comforted her for a few days before relegating her to the pool of pets around the house. I didn't do that because I had learned a fuller relationship was possible. Consequently, I have been rewarded with another intensely close, special relationship with an animal. I feel fortunate, indeed, that I still have half of Cindy's life ahead of me and our future experiences will keep my memory pile tall.

I've deliberately accentuated the differences between Cleo and Cindy, dogs that have entirely different personalities but that formed the same type of intense bond with me. Yet some of the similarities are equally striking and I will describe just one here.

Because of the intense summer heat, Judy began taking Cindy for her long walk before breakfast rather than later in the hot morning. After one such recent outing, I noticed Cindy panting heavily inside the door a full ten minutes after the walk. She seemed completely wiped out. There was water in the next room and I could have adopted the attitude that, if she wanted it badly enough, she could go get it. I was, after all, trying to enjoy my breakfast.

But I didn't do that. I filled a bowl with cool water and placed it between her legs. You will recall that Cindy is a finicky eater and drinker who prefers to wait awhile before satisfying her needs. Not that time. She eagerly lapped up that delicious liquid that was, to borrow a commercial saying, good to the very last drop.

I removed the bowl and returned to my breakfast while I caught the news on CNN. For some reason I glanced at Cindy. Although she was still lying in the same place, she had recovered noticeably and—this is important—was staring at me with her ears in the alert position. I said something to her but she didn't look away or change expression. Instead, she continued staring at me for quite some time. It was the same type of stare, described earlier, that I had received from young Cleo on one of our trips. Cleo had been *studying* me then and Cindy was doing the same now. I had done something nice for her and she was trying to understand me because of it. Our already close relationship had moved up a notch, maybe two or three. I'm convinced Cindy, like Cleo, was using social intelligence to consciously and deliberately understand her caring human.

George Page in *Inside the Animal Mind* quotes internationally renowned primatologist Jane Goodall as saying you can't look into the eyes of a chimpanzee and not see intelligence. I feel the same way about Cindy's eyes, and Cleo's. Those eyes show intelligent understanding, contrary to what so many still believe. Our dogs can't understand our words except for a few commands and Cindy's impressive array of vocalizations convey only a few needs and emotions. So communication by eye contact is immensely important in a dog-human relationship.

I never knew this before Cleo and Cindy, which means I missed the opportunity to understand and appreciate and communicate fully with the nearly dozen dogs I'd owned earlier. It's taken me most of a lifetime to become a connoisseur of dogs and my other pets as well. It took a couple special relationships and some thinking and some reading to expect more in my relationship with pets. I hope some of my readers will profit from my experiences.

For nine months after Cleo's death, I tossed all sorts of jottings, Internet printouts, photos, newspaper clippings, books and videos onto my memory pile. It became so tall it began to topple over, so I devoted a little time each morning before breakfast to organizing the material into readable form. I hoped to have a working draft by the first anniversary of Cleo's death, but it took much longer. When I finally completed a very rough draft, I sat down and read it nonstop from beginning to end. Oh, it was a marvelous experience. There was my whole life with Cleo and Cindy (to that point) in *unforgettable* print. I was so glad I decided to do it.

I don't believe there's ever been a time in my life when I wasn't working on one writing project or another. I'm compulsive about putting things down on paper, and my family and friends know that. When some of them began asking me what I was working on at the time, I felt a little silly telling them I was writing up my relationships with a couple dogs. I usually mentioned some other project so they wouldn't laugh at me. Eventually, however, I told them the truth and was amazed at the responses. Although I received an occasional incredulous stare, most people said it was a great idea. And they seemed to mean it. Judy made me promise to let her see it as soon as possible—she loves Cindy and loved Cleo as much as I.

These unexpected responses were consistent with the enormous outpouring of condolences I received at Cleo's death and the widespread interest in dogs I found; it was always there for anyone to notice, but I never had. A large proportion of the American population harbors very tender feelings for canine pets, both their own and others'. I began to wonder whether they might like to read my story.

I have no idea what the future will bring, but I'm looking forward to it. Cindy's a great dog, still in her prime, and I've protected the memory of Cleo the best I can. They say dogs are man's best friends. They won't get an argument from me.

# ABOUT THE AUTHOR

Jack Dempsey has been leading several lives for decades.

His wife and three kids have provided endless hours of sanity, relaxation, stimulation and shared interests. There has never been a time when pets of all types didn't share in family life.

Public health has provided Jack with his primary source of income for most of his life. To that end, he earned a doctorate in public health from Johns Hopkins. He also is a Phi Beta Kappa member, received a presidential certificate of appreciation for contributions to the White House Conference on Families, and received a teacher-of-the-year award at Johns Hopkins' School of Public Health.

Jack and wife Judy have been animal lovers, nature enthusiasts and wildlife photographers throughout their marriage. Together they produced a photo calendar of the Delmarva Peninsula featuring waterfowl and other wildlife.

Jack's professional and hobbyist publications include four books, magazine articles, journal publications and feature newspaper articles. "However," Jack maintains, "this fifth book about two of my dogs is the most rewarding work of love in my life."

Jack now lives and writes in semi-retirement on North Carolina's Outer Banks with Judy, a dog, four cats and, outside, bird feeders everywhere, fish in a pond and visiting deer, foxes, raccoons, squirrels and rabbits.